CW00338410

ARE YOU PSYCHIC?

Tests & games to measure your powers

ARE YOU PSYCHIC?

**Tests & games
to measure your powers**

**HANS J EYSENCK &
CARL SARGENT**

PRION

ALS?

This edition published
in Great Britain 1996 by PRION
32–34 Gordon House Road,
London NW5 1LP

A catalogue record of this book can be obtained
from the British Library

ISBN 1-85375-195-2

Text illustrations by Sally Maltby
Cover design by Tamasin Cole
Cover image *Stars* from Galaxy Picture Library

Typeset by Books Unlimited (Nottm), Mansfield NG19 7QZ
Printed and bound in Great Britain by
Biddles Ltd., Guildford & Kings Lynn

Contents

Introduction: You and your Psi

What is psi?
There have always been people who have claimed to have had psychic experiences. And yet, though no one denies that the human mind is a powerful tool with wide-ranging abilities, some of these abilities are hotly debated. Can people really have ESP – extra sensory perception? Is there such a thing as mind-over-matter? It is these two abilities – ESP and mind-over-matter or psychokinesis, PK – that are covered by the term *psi* (short for psychical).

But what do ESP and PK mean? PK is the action of the human mind on matter directly, without any known physical force being involved. We've all heard about metal-bending, which is an example of PK. But in this book we are mainly concerned with ESP: getting information about other people or events without using our five senses or by being able to work things out logically. Surveys show that most of us believe in ESP, and also that we have almost all had at least one experience which we feel involved ESP. As public interest in the subject has grown, so has the demand for sound scientific evidence about ESP. People don't want sensationalized and unreliable reports of alleged miracles which have little to do with their experiences. But neither will they be fobbed off by doctrinaire claims from sceptical scientists that parapsychology (as the scientific study of psi is known) is all error, hoax and fraud. This book is for such people: people who would like to try direct exploration of psi, either seriously or for fun, but hopefully both. But if you're sceptical, you can still find this book challenging and useful. The challenge is simply this: before being so sure that psi events don't exist, dabble with some experiments. You just might be surprised; it wouldn't be the first time a sceptic had to change his mind.

The tests in this book do vary from the preliminary, fun-and-games type at one end of the spectrum to computer tests at the other. But there is absolutely no need for you to have any statistical expertise or any particular scientific knowledge to be able to make the most of this book.

Evidence for psi

One kind of evidence for the reality of psi is the performances of *exceptional individuals*. These are 'psychics', the Psi Stars as we have dubbed them – people whose psi powers have been studied for long periods of time by a considerable number of researchers. One such person was the Victorian medium D. D. Home (a splendid biography of him by Elizabeth Jenkins, *The Shadow and the Light*, has been published). Literally hundreds of witnesses independently testified to Home's PK powers: he levitated himself and raised other people and objects into the air; he plucked burning coals from fires and held them with no injury to himself, and placed these coals on the heads of seance sitters; on more than one occasion, avalanches of spirit rappings occurred on such a scale that witnesses feared the very house would fall down. His powers were studied and validated by the scientist Sir William Crookes, and by many others. He was never caught cheating (although he certainly never lacked enemies) and he never accepted money for seances which were often conducted in bright light, although he did publish exposés of fraudulent mediumistic practices. In the century since his death not a single sceptical attack on him of any real merit has appeared. As William Crookes insists, to reject the testimony about him is to reject any human testimony whatsoever.

A more contemporary Psi Star is the American medical student Bill Delmore, studied by the Institute of Para-psychology in North Carolina and other institutes in the 1970s. Delmore has two major claims to fame: first, that he was successful with almost every psi test given to him; and second, he knew when his psi was working. The *pièce de résistance* for Delmore was his performance in guessing sealed-up playing cards;

occasionally, Delmore would get a strong feeling that his guess had been correct. In one major experiment, of his 25 'confidence calls' Delmore scored 20 correct; clearly something amazing was happening. There are 52 cards in a pack; the chance of a simple guess being correct by coincidence is 1 in 52; but Delmore scored four correct out of every five. We do not need to have any statistical knowledge to see that this is astonishing.

Card-guessing, electronic testing for ESP by machine, PK tests – Delmore was successful with everything thrown at him. It's normal for researchers, given such a Psi Star, to state that the odds against his score being due to chance are so many billions to one; but with Delmore, it's not worth bothering, for the word 'billion' would have to be repeated too many times.

Another Psi Star of past years is the Trinidadian Lalsingh Harribance. Harribance has a talent for psychometry – obtaining information about people and events from material objects associated with them. The test most commonly used with him has been guessing the sex of people shown in concealed photographs, at which he has been phenomenally successful.

As an example, in 1970, Harribance was tested at the Psychical Research Foundation in North Carolina by psychologist Bob Morris and colleagues. In one series of experiments, Harribance – seated quietly in one room – guessed the sex of people shown in pictures being displayed separately in another unconnected room and randomly ordered male/female. Each test run was 10 guesses, and he completed 105 runs. Instead of getting the chance average of five correct per run (10 guesses, 50 per cent chance of being correct with each guess by chance alone), Harribance averaged just under 6.5. The odds against this score exceed a million to one. And, immediately after, Harribance was tested using ESP cards, and produced a 50,000 to 1 result for this! Other researchers have obtained results just as good with him, and checks on his brain wave activity have confirmed the classical finding of high ESP scores being associated with relaxation, lack of external distraction and a 'quiet mind'.

Psychological factors

Certainly, more Psi Stars could be added to this list. But other important sources of evidence are experiments where groups of *ordinary subjects* are tested; and certain patterns of operation of ESP emerge when the results of several studies are compared. Most of these patterns concern the psychology of ESP. For example, numerous experiments have compared ESP test scores with measurements of extroversion (the tendency to be impulsive, sociable, lively and so on). Results from 22 experiments conducted by 13 different experimenters in many different countries have shown that extroverts score higher in ESP tests than introverts. One on one occasion has the reverse picture emerged clearly, and this can be dismissed as the statistical exception that proves the rule.

As another example, results from 17 experiments

conducted by 10 different experimenters in several different countries have shown that subjects who believe in, or at least accept the possibility of, ESP score higher in ESP tests than people who just don't believe it, while the reverse has never been observed strongly. This is clear evidence that belief can boost ESP scores.

The value of pattern results

It may be that these 'pattern results' are the best kind of evidence for psi, even though they're not as dramatic at first sight as the Psi Star evidence. They can be carefully checked and repeated and so hopefully eliminate experimental error or idiosyncratic effects.

If the pattern effects are consistent then they may not just be evidence for the existence of psi – they're also telling us something about the psychology of psi. But we might be badly misled about the way it may function in people who are not Psi Stars. If we only studied individual Psi Stars our picture of the psychology of psi and how psi fits in with personality and behaviour might be misleading: exceptional people do tend to show exceptional and idiosyncratic psi effects. A better understanding of the workings of psi in your life must surely be gained by studying these pattern results.

One final point about the pattern evidence seems obvious. If we read an account of the metal-bending PK feats of, say, the French PK Psi Star Jean-Paul Girard – for example, his remarkable ability of bending objects in sealed glass tubes – we are most impressed, but we can't do much more than just be impressed, unless we are lucky enough to be able to work with him. Naturally, for most of us, this isn't a practical possibility: Girards are a rare commodity. But if you are interested in personality and ESP, you can conduct your own tests on friends and relatives. Give them the Psi questionnaire, test them for ESP using one or more of the tests in this book and see if they really *do* match up. Pattern evidence comes from studies of ordinary people. Such experiments don't work on every occasion (no experiment in social science ever does), but they work often enough to show that there is something which cannot be put down to coincidence alone. To conclude, the historical evidence (as with D. D. Home) is very powerful. But psi is much more interesting – and fun – if you can see it work at first hand.

1

'Are You a Psi Star?'

Testing and the Psi Questionnaire
It is a good idea to complete the psi questionnaire *now*,
before you begin any of the tests. Fill the answers in,
but don't work out your score. Conduct some psi tests,
and when you have your first results, come back to the
questionnaire, score it and see if the answers concord
with the test scores: do you show evidence of psi abilities in one or the other, or both? It is useful to have a
Psi questionnaire score which was obtained before any
ESP results were known. That way, your answers
would not be subtly biased by knowing about your ESP
scores. The questionnaire is divided into three parts:
sheep and goats; personality and interests; and mystery
and imagination. Sheep and goats has been adapted
from a questionnaire sent to members of the Society for
Psychical Research in 1982, the SPR centenary year.

In each section, you are asked a series of questions
which may be answered Yes/?/No. Circle the appro-

priate answer each time but avoid marking '?' if possible. If you do not want to mark the book, record the question numbers and answers on a separate sheet of paper.

Work through the questions fairly quickly and write down the first answer that occurs to you, rather than thinking about the questions for too long. Don't dwell on the precise wording of each question: if some of them seem to be repetitive, remember that there are good reasons for asking the same things in slightly different ways. It may not always be easy to answer the questions in Part 3, since some of them are necessarily vague; but try not to give ? answers.

Scoring keys are provided after each section.

Part 1: Sheep and Goats

1 Do you believe in the existence of ESP, extra-sensory perception? Yes ? No
2 Do you believe that you have had personal experience of ESP? Yes ? No
3 Do you believe that it is possible to gain information about the future before it happens, in ways which do not depend on rational prediction or normal sensory channels? Yes ? No
4 Do you believe that you have had at least one hunch that turned out to be correct and which (you believe) was not just a coincidence? Yes ? No
5 Do you recall having had at least one dream which came true which (you believe) was not just a coincidence? Yes ? No

6 Do you believe that it is possible to gain information about the thoughts, feelings or circumstances of another person, in a way which does not depend on rational prediction or normal sensory channels? Yes ? No

7 Do you believe that you have had at least one experience which involved telepathy between yourself and another person? Yes ? No

8 Has there ever been an occasion in your life when you have had the strong feeling that you have been in the same place or situation before, even though you had never actually been there or were experiencing the event for the first time in 'real life'? Yes ? No

9 Has there ever been an occasion in your life when you felt that your 'self' or 'centre of consciousness' was in a spatial location outside of your body? Yes ? No

10 Do you believe in the existence of PK (psychokinesis), that is, the direct effect of mind on a physical object or system, without the mediation of any known energy? Yes ? No

11 Do you believe that you have personally exerted PK on at least one occasion? Yes ? No

12 Have you ever witnessed an occurrence of PK (non-recurrent) which had as its source another person? Yes ? No

13 Do you believe in the existence of poltergeists (a poltergeist being an apparent 'spirit' which causes rappings, bangs, and other PK effects recurrently)? Yes ? No

14 Do you believe that poltergeist activity, or other forms of persistent PK activity, have occurred in your presence at some time in the past? Yes ? No

15 Do you believe that psychic healing occurs? Yes ? No

16 Have you ever witnessed or experienced what you believe to be psychic healing performed upon either yourself or another person? Yes ? No

17 Do you believe that you have any talent for psychic healing Yes ? No

18 Do you believe that you have or might have above-average ESP ability? Yes ? No

19 Do you believe that you have or might have above-average PK ability? Yes ? No

20 Do you believe that, on the whole, the world is better off with psi (ESP and PK) phenomena than without them? Yes ? No

21 Do you read books and articles on parapsychology fairly often? Yes ? No

22 Do you believe in life after death? Yes ? No

23 Do you believe that some people (*mediums*) can contact spirits of the dead? Yes ? No

24 Have you ever consulted a medium? Yes ? No

25 Do you believe that you yourself possess mediumistic gifts? Yes ? No

26 Do you believe in the occurrence of reincarnation? Yes ? No

27 Do you believe that you have experienced what seems to be a genuine memory of a previous life? Yes ? No

28 Do you read articles or books about religious matters fairly often? Yes ? No
29 Do you read the Bible or another major religious text (such as the Koran) at least occasionally? Yes ? No
30 Do you attend religious gatherings at least moderately frequently – say, once a month? Yes ? No
31 Do you believe in the God of Christianity? Yes ? No
32 Do you believe in a God, but not necessarily the God of Christianity? Yes ? No
33 Have you ever felt in some way the presence of God, or higher power? Yes ? No
34 Do you believe in the existence of some sort of 'group mind', or 'collective unconscious'? Yes ? No

Answers to Part 1

Score 2 points for every 'yes' and 1 point for every '?'.

0–26: Welcome to the goats. Your view of life is sceptical – how can psychic phenomena *really* exist? Although you might not think it, your scores are affected by your attitude. The surprising thing is that goats not only score badly, they score *negatively*! It's almost as if you try not to score. Try some of the tests and see if this is the case. You might like also to test your less sceptical friends.

27–40: You just can't decide! Sometimes you're convinced, and other times not. Concentrate on developing the positive side of your mind (read our accounts of psi events in Chapter 2). Admit to the possibilities of psi and see how this affects your scores.

41–68: You need no encouragement in this. As a sheep you're raring to go. You should try the more complicated tests, once you have mastered the simple ones – make things tough for yourself.

You may be interested in breaking down this section of the questionnaire into its four components as follows:

General belief:	Questions 1, 3, 6, 10, 13, 15
Acceptance and interest:	Questions 17, 18, 19, 20, 21
Personal experience:	Questions 2, 4, 5, 7, 8, 9, 11, 12, 14, 16, 25
Survival after death, and religion:	Questions 22, 23, 24, 26–34

Add up the scores in each subsection. Compare the scores in each one. Typically, we find that people scoring high in one section, score high in the others also.

Part 2: Personality and interests

1 Are you fairly talkative when you are with a group of people? Yes ? No
2 Do you save regularly? Yes ? No
3 Would you rather read the sports page than the editorial leaders in a newspaper? Yes ? No

4 When you go on a trip do you like to plan routes and timetables carefully? Yes ? No

5 Do you like work that involves action rather than profound thought and study? Yes ? No

6 Are you normally on time for appointments? Yes ? No

7 Do you often buy things on impulse? Yes ? No

8 Do you like to have time to be alone with your thoughts? Yes ? No

9 Do you (would you) enjoy fast driving? Yes ? No

10 Do you hate being with a crowd who play practical jokes on one another? Yes ? No

11 Have you occasionally 'played sick' to avoid an unpleasant responsibility? Yes ? No

12 Do you lock up your house carefully at night? Yes ? No

13 Can you usually let yourself go and have a good time at a party? Yes ? No

14 Do you often try to find the underlying motives for the actions of other people? Yes ? No

15 Are you generally unconcerned about the future? Yes ? No

16 If you were making a business enquiry would you rather write than discuss it on the telephone? Yes ? No

17 Do you prefer activities that just happen to those planned in advance? Yes ? No

18 Do you usually answer a personal letter immediately after you have received it? Yes ? No

19 Would you prefer a job involving change, travel and variety even though risky and insecure? Yes ? No

20 Do you know what you will be doing on your next holiday? Yes ? No

21 Do you like to tell jokes and stories to groups of friends? Yes ? No

22 When buying things, do you usually examine the guarantee? Yes ? No

23 Would you agree that an element of risk adds spice to life? Yes ? No

24 Do you prefer to 'sleep on it' before making decisions? Yes ? No

25 Did you occasionally play truant in your schooldays? Yes ? No

26 Do you frequently become so involved with a question or problem that you have to keep thinking about it until you arrive at a satisfactory solution? Yes ? No

27 Do you often get involved in things you later prefer to opt out of? Yes ? No

28 Do you enjoy solitary activities such as playing patience and solving cross-word puzzles? Yes ? No

29 Do you think it is a waste of time to formulate plans for an ideal society or Utopia? Yes ? No

30 Do you set an alarm clock if you have to be up at a particular time in the morning? Yes ? No

31 Are you easily irritated by things that are out of place? Yes ? No

32 Do you make your own decisions regardless of what other people say? Yes ? No

33 Do you blush more than most people? Yes ? No

34 Would you say that you have a high opinion of yourself? Yes ? No

35 Do you usually blame yourself if something goes wrong with your personal relationships? Yes ? No

36 Do you feel comfortable if your home gets untidy? Yes ? No

37 Do you often wish you were someone else? Yes ? No

38 If you have made an awkward social error can you forget it easily? Yes ? No

39 Do you believe that your personality was laid down firmly by the things that happened to you as a child, so that there isn't much you can do to change it? Yes ? No

40 Are you rarely troubled by feelings of guilt? Yes ? No

41 Do you keep very careful accounts of all the money you've spent? Yes ? No

42 Do you usually feel that you can accomplish the things you want to? Yes ? No

43 Do you often catch yourself apologizing when you are not really at fault? Yes ? No

44 Can you relax quite easily when sitting or lying down? Yes ? No

45 Do you often feel that you have little influence over the things that happen to you? Yes ? No

46 Is it easy for you to forget the things that you have done wrong? Yes ? No

47 Are there some members of your family who make you feel that you are not good enough? Yes ? No

48 Would you walk under a ladder on the street rather than go out of your way to detour round it? Yes ? No

49 Would you be troubled by feelings of inadequacy if you had to make a speech? Yes ? No

50 If you see a game that you would like to be good at are you usually able to acquire the necessary skill to enjoy it? Yes ? No

51 Do you believe that bad behaviour will always be punished in the long run? Yes ? No

52 If you have done something morally wrong can you quickly forget it and direct your thoughts to the future? Yes ? No

53 As a child were you afraid of the dark? Yes ? No

54 Do you think your personality is attractive to the opposite sex? Yes ? No

55 Do you often feel restless as if you want something but you do not know what? Yes ? No

56 Can you drop off to sleep quite easily at night? Yes ? No

57 Are most of the things you do geared to pleasing other people? Yes ? No

58 Have you as much will power as the next person? Yes ? No

59 Do you often do jobs yourself rather than trust someone else to do it properly? Yes ? No

60 Can you easily disregard little mistakes and inaccuracies? Yes ? No

Answers to Part 2

Questions 1 to 30 inclusive measure the personality variable of *extroversion*. Every time you circled 'yes' to an odd-numbered question (1, 3, 5, 7, etc.) score 2 points. Every time you circled 'no' to an even-numbered question (2, 4, 6, 8, etc.) score 2 points. '?' merits 1 point each time.

36–60: You certainly are an extrovert – impulsive, risk-taking and generally sociable. You may be using your psi ability already without realizing it. Scores you get in tests should be good, but try the techniques explained in Chapter 3 to improve your scores. Repress your exuberant, expressive side long enough to try the ganzfeld experiments in Chapter 7.

25–35: You fluctuate between extrovert and introvert tendencies. You can see both sides of the situation quite clearly, and you're pretty level-headed when making decisions – you may even be a little sceptical about the existence of psi. Try the games and enjoy them. You may feel sufficiently encouraged to try the more complicated ones. Your potential is good.

0–24: An introverted, withdrawn nature such as yours is not naturally suited to good psi scores and you probably have a long way to go before you are a Psi Star. Try some of the easier tests. You may do better than you expected. Make sure you are comfortable – in

friendly surroundings. There is every chance that this
may boost your scores and your confidence.

Questions 31 to 60 inclusive measure the personality
variable of *anxiety*, also known as neuroticism or emotional instability. Every time you circled 'yes' to an
odd-numbered question score 2 points; 'no' to an even-
numbered question scores 2 points. As before, every '?'
scores 1 point.

36–60: Anxiety is not the way to a high psi score. If you
are to succeed, you must try to relax – follow the
techniques for progressive relaxation. Highly anxious
people, with their low self-esteem and lack of
independence, are not the best subjects for psi experiments – in fact you probably won't even want to participate. Take heart! You never know what you are
capable of.

25–35: Your evenness of temperament may be reflected
in scores that do not deviate dramatically from the
average. You, along with your more anxious friends,
would benefit also from a course of relaxation – why not
also try the word and picture games. Best of all, try
them after doing some tests and then conduct more
tests after the exercises.

0–24: You are one of that lucky breed – the emotionally
stable! Like your extrovert friends (you may also be an
extrovert too), your psi scores should reflect this, being

higher than average. See if you can improve your scores
still further.

Part 3: Mystery and Imagination

1 I can remember clearly at least one thing which
   happened to me when I was two years old or
   younger. Yes ? No
2 When I was a child, I could imagine I was flying
   with such vividness that I felt as if I actually did fly.
   Yes ? No
3 As a child I enjoyed fairytales. Yes ? No
4 As an adult I still enjoy fairytales. Yes ? No
5 As a child, I would at times pretend and *in some
   sense believe* I was someone else such as a fairytale
   character (Snow White, Peter Pan or some such), a
   prince or princess, an orphan, etc. Yes ? No
6 As an adult I occasionally *pretend* I am someone
   else. Yes ? No
7 I would like to be hypnotized (or have enjoyed
   being hypnotized). Yes ? No
8 I recall my dreams easily. Yes ? No
9 If I wish, I am usually able to finish or even change
   a dream after I awaken. Yes ? No
10 At times just before I fall asleep I experience vivid
   images. Yes ? No
11 If I remember a significant event in my life, in
   addition to thinking about it I can re-experience
   it: I can see again what I saw then, hear again
   the sounds, voices, etc.; feel the emotions and

sensations I felt then. Yes ? No

12 If I try and conjure up a mental image in my 'mind's eye' of a friend, I find that easy to do. Yes ? No

13 I generally recall whole dreams – with stories and series of images – rather than just fragments. Yes ? No

14 When I was a child I had an imaginary companion (or companions) such as an imagined person, animal or object which I talked to, shared feelings with, or took along with me. Yes ? No

15 I greatly enjoy daydreaming. Yes ? No

16 If I closed my eyes and tried to imagine holding a baby, or a cat or dog, in my lap, I could easily feel the weight and warmth of the creature. Yes ? No

17 If I try to imagine a scene from a favourite film, and close my eyes, I can see it really vividly in my mind's eye. Yes ? No

18 If I'm reading a book, I find I can easily identify with at least some of the characters – feel what they are feeling. Yes ? No

19 I can 'lose myself' in some physical activity like dancing or running quite easily. Yes ? No

20 I like wide-open windows. Yes ? No

Answers to Part 3

This part of the questionnaire is the most experimental: we don't know exactly what to expect from it. Give yourself 2 points for each 'yes' answer and 1 for each '?'. The range of scores is 0 to 40 points.

27–40: What richly detailed fantasy world do you inhabit? Do you have trouble putting your feet on the ground? With your flights of imagination you will find the picture tests (Chapters 7 – 9) will be of interest and rather more challenging.

13–26: With your occasional flashes of insight, you could find that your score varies according to your mood. By keeping a diary, you might find a significant correlation between the two.

0–12: Down-to-earth and practical – no nonsense for you: your feet rarely leave the ground. Don't dismiss psi just yet. Try some of the easier games. Apart from anything else, you might find them fun!

2

Principles of ESP Testing

Types of test
There are some simple basic terms used in ESP experiments which will appear throughout this book. The first is *subject:* the person who is attempting to use ESP in the experiment, by 'guessing' at cards, pictures, etc. The *experimenter* is the person who is running the test, the person who collects the results, prepares the test and so on. Next, there are the *targets*. These are the objects (cards, pictures, etc.) that the subject is trying to detect by ESP.

Clairvoyance
The simplest kind of ESP test involves these three elements only. The subject is asked by the experimenter to 'guess' the nature of the targets; if the experiment is successful, the ESP is between the subject and the

targets and is called mind-to-matter ESP or *clairvoyance* (ESP of events or objects). A possible example of this is the operation of certain proclaimed 'psychic detectives', who locate lost items of jewellery or (more morbidly) undiscovered bodies in murder cases and so on. This is less familiar than mind-to-mind ESP or *telepathy*, with which we deal next.

Telepathy

A telepathy experiment brings in a fourth factor: the agent or *sender*. The sender is shown the targets and the subject tries to pick up from the mind of the sender what the targets are. Thoughtful readers will have realized already that one cannot be certain if the subject (assuming he is successful) is picking up the targets via the mind of the sender or directly; clairvoyance can be an explanation of the results in a telepathy experiment. So that we don't get bogged down in technical details, we shall use the term 'telepathy experiment' for all experiments where the sender is involved and the clairvoyance possibility ignored.

Precognition

The third and final kind of ESP experiment has the usual components – subject, experimenter and targets, and maybe a sender too – but differs in a crucial respect from ordinary clairvoyance and telepathy studies. This, the *precognition* experiment, tests for ESP of events which have not yet occurred when the subject makes his guesses: the targets do not yet exist. This puzzling type of ESP *of future* events may be the most challenging and exciting effect to be studied.

Principles of testing

A good ESP experiment, as any experiment, should be conducted using sound test methods. The four essentials of procedure are:

1 Eliminate sensory cues.
2 A subject in an ESP experiment should not be able to deduce anything about the targets by logic: the targets should be random.
3 The results should be recorded accurately and objectively.
4 We should be able to test our results against some constant measure. In this book, as in the laboratory, we have used a measure against *chance*. The chance of an event happening at random can be calculated. If the event happens more often than chance would predict we have an *objective measure* of the possibility of ESP having played a part.

Why are these elements important? We shall take them one by one.

Sensory cues

ESP is the acquiring of information about people or events without involving the known senses, so we must eliminate the possibility of any of our five senses providing the information. In *all* types of experiment we must shield the target from the subject; in telepathy experiments we must shield the sender also; and in certain experiments other precautions are needed.

The importance of sensory cues in ESP experiments can vary. There is evidence that unusually sensitive persons may be able to pick up very subtle cues – whispers from a sender in a telepathy experiment which are made quite involuntarily can be picked up by such people even when observers are satisfied that nothing audible is happening.

Random targets

Imagine that someone dreams of the death of Uncle Fred, and at the time they wake up Uncle Fred is indeed dying. Is this ESP? If Uncle Fred was 45, in the best of health, then quite possibly. But if Uncle Fred was 92, bedridden and suffering from a terminal illness, most people wouldn't think that ESP was involved. The rule is: if something could have been expected, rationally or logically predicted, then the evidence for ESP is weak. If some entirely unexpected information is picked up, the evidence for ESP being involved is stronger.

Recording the results

Unless machine testing is used, the results of an ESP experiment will be recorded by a human being, and human beings are fallible. Mistakes in recording results *must* occur, although trained experimenters make them very rarely. It is impossible to eliminate mistakes completely; but things can be arranged so that they don't matter. Game 8 on page 79 is a good example of how this should be done.

An objective measure for SP

It is essential for any serious or even half serious ESP test to use an objective measurement of the results, and all the tests in this book do. In most cases, when people are discussing experiences they have had which they feel may have involved ESP, a sceptic may say, 'That's just coincidence' and very often one simply cannot argue the case for ESP.

However, if we can obtain some *measure* of ESP, we can make a great advance. We can work out the likelihood of any measured score in an ESP experiment being due to coincidence – or, more precisely, the laws of chance. The logic of how we can do this is very simple and requires no statistical expertise.

The laws of chance

Let us have a look at a card-guessing game. It will help to explain the laws of chance.

There are 52 cards in a pack, 26 red and 26 black. If we are trying to guess the colour, then for each card we have a 50 per cent probability of being correct using guesswork alone. So, by the laws of chance, we would expect on average to get about 26 (50 per cent of 52) correct if we guessed through the pack. Here is the first key idea: the *chance average*. This is a measure of what the term 'coincidence' means.

Deciding what is chance

What if someone scores 30 correct? 35? 40? Is ESP involved? To answer this question, the second and final important idea enters the picture – that of *scatter*. If we only guessed the answer each time (no ESP), we would not expect to score exactly 26 correct every time. The average score for a series of tests would be very close to 26, but individual test scores would vary around the average – 22, 27, 21, 23, 29, 28…Again, this notion of scatter around the average is easily grasped. There are mathematical and statistical equations which tell us

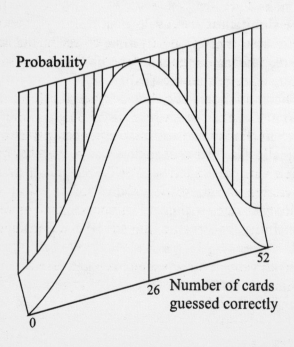

exactly how much scatter we would expect by chance, and the central point is that the further away from the average we go, the less likely a score is to occur by chance. A score of 30 (or more) correct out of 52 is not particularly unexpected; the deviation from the expected score (of 26) is only four and such a deviation (or larger) would be expected around once every three tests. Clearly *not* unusual. A score of 35 would be another matter: the deviation of nine (or larger) would be expected by chance only once every 55 tests. A score of 40 would be extremely unusual: a chance expectation of only once every 1100 tests.

How significant are results?

These results show neatly the central principle, but where is the dividing line? Where does one say that the result shows evidence of ESP?

There is an arbitrary but consistent rule of thumb in statistical science which psychologists and parapsychologists use. If the chance probability is 1 in 20 or smaller (five per cent chance, or a probability of 0.05, which can be written as $P = 0.05$ or less), then one concludes that there is evidence for an effect which is not just due to chance. Of course, the smaller the probability, or P value, the stronger the influence of ESP.

In our games and experiments we have selected three commonly used probability levels and interpreted them as follows:

Probability   1 in 20 or 0.05   some psi effect
                   1 in 100 or 0.01   good psi effect
                   1 in 1000 or 0.001   excellent psi effect

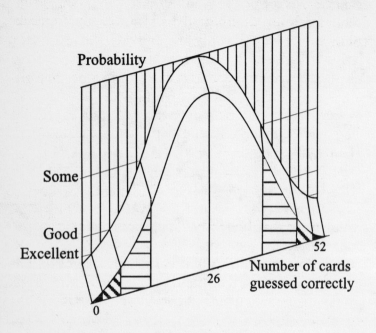

If you want to work out the significance of your scores for yourself, the Appendices contain all the necessary information for you to do so.

If you don't want to do this, there are also score keys for which you should do the specified number of tests each time (if you are using the tables to score, you can do as many tests as you like). They incorporate all the information from the tables but are easier to read.

For each test, you will have a number of guesses or throws and a number of correct scores or hits.

Example: For a 1 in 2 test
Look for your number of hits in the appropriate column.

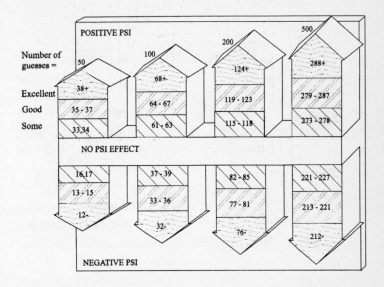

POSITIVE PSI

Number of guesses =

	50	100	200	500
Excellent	38+	68+	124+	288+
Good	35 - 37	64 - 67	119 - 123	279 - 287
Some	33,34	61 - 63	115 - 118	273 - 278

NO PSI EFFECT

	16,17	37 - 39	82 - 85	221 - 227
	13 - 15	33 - 36	77 - 81	213 - 221
	12-	32-	76-	212-

NEGATIVE PSI

There are occasions when we use different methods of scoring – for example, the rank sum test (see p.97) – but you'll find a key to help you interpret your results as before.

By now, you may have guessed that it is possible to score significantly lower as well as higher than chance. What does this mean?

Psi missing

You will see that for each probability column, a low value is given as well as a high one. A very *low* score may show ESP just as a very *high* score does. This may be puzzling at first sight, but it can be seen easily enough that if someone tries to guess a series of cards and just goes on and on getting them wrong that *something* odd is happening. This negative psi, or 'psi missing' as we shall call it may be to the Psi tests what bad luck is in real life! It may be that we fail to observe such an effect in real life as we tend not to notice a *lack* of interesting coincidences. All we can say for now is that psi missing is favoured by scepticism, boredom and fatigue – when you have tested for this in Chapter 9, you may find a correlation between these factors and psi missing.

Group scoring

You may find that in the competitive games (Chapter 4) the individual scores are not significant. Try adding together the scores and see whether or not they are collectively significant – this often seems to be the case. It may mean that psi abilities of individuals are too weak to show up by themselves, but such abilities will show up when scores are combined this way. This highlights very small psi effects. If this is the case, you should try to stimulate better psi, as described in Chapter 3, or do further tests to find out which of you have the psi ability.

Using the tables (Appendix 1)

Tables I–IV are all used in the same way: in every test you will be deciding between a fixed number of options, and it is this number that determines which table you use. If, for example, you are guessing the colour of cards in a pack, then you will have two options – red and black – and so you use Table I for 1 in 2 tests. If, on the other hand, you are guessing dice faces in a PK test, you will use Table III for 1 in 6. Table V is a list of random numbers which you will need each time you select a number or object at random. Full instructions are given at the head of the table.

Look for your number of guesses in the left-hand column. Now check across the probability columns: if your score is equal to or higher than a number in one of the positive columns, or equal to or lower than those in the negative columns, then you have a significant score at that level.

As your number of options increases, it follows that you will need to carry out rather more tests to find a significant result.

Scoring significant differences

In some of the tests, you are asked to compare two sets of scores, either between different players or scores from the same player at different times. This is done in cases where you are investigating the effects of various factors on your psi-ability such as time of day (same player) or introversion/extroversion (different players). By working out the significance of the difference between scores, you have a measure of the strength of these effects. Each time we provide the appropriate key, but you can score results using the tables as follows.

Combine the number of guesses made and look for this in the left-hand column. Then, look for the difference between the scores in the right-hand three columns. These are interpreted essentially the same as before, but this time you will be getting significant deviations. For example, if you are scoring for two players on the same test, a deviation that falls in the 0.01 column (that number or higher) indicates that there is a probability of 1 in 100 of this happening and you can say that this is a *good* score. Differences which are less than the 0.05 value are not significant.

Sometimes, figures may not be shown in the 'Deviation' columns. If this is so, it is because the deviations *above* and *below* chance needed for a significant result are not the same; only symmetrical deviation scores are shown. This usually only happens with a very small number of guesses. However, if you need to check a difference score with such a small number of guesses, check the difference between the chance average score and the *positive* psi score; if the difference between your psi test scores is the same as, or exceeds, one or more of these chance v. positive psi differences, there is a significant difference between the test scores.

Finally, some deviation scores are fractional – for obvious reasons. When checking for significant differences, round these *up*.

Fun and games, and moving on

The tests in the following chapters vary in the rigidness of their experimental conditions. The earlier ones, which we call games, do not comprise all the elements of a scientific test, and are intended primarily as warm-up exercises for the later tests, which we call experiments. They will get you in the habit of setting up the tests and of scoring them as accurately as possible. Use them also as party games; they are fun to do.

Many researchers find it valuable to conduct a series of tests – starting with loose, free and easy conditions, and when subjects have got used to the test and feel comfortable, slowly tightening the conditions to end with a highly controlled psi test. In this way they build the confidence of the subjects and their familiarity with the test procedures. The American 'father of parapsychology', J. B. Rhine, used to do this with card tests for ESP; and researchers looking at possible PK in seances have learned that the recording of paranormal sounds and forces requires the *gradual* bringing in of equipment, so that people become accustomed to the test environment first.

It is helpful to build up confidence in this way, but don't confuse the different types of test! With loose tests, any results which suggest ESP may be the result of sensory clues, or whatever, distorting the results. They provide evidence only of *possible* psi. The controlled tests provide the stronger evidence. You can follow our trail of pre-set tests using the conditions we suggest and scoring from the keys, or you can go it alone and use your imagination to devise other tests.

The chapter that follows describes various preparation exercises that you should try before starting the games.

3

Developing and Stimulating ESP

We are concerned here with learning how to increase your psi. There are two central themes in the games and exercises we suggest. The first is that there is now overwhelming evidence to show that subjects score best in ESP tests when they are *relaxed*, mentally and physically. This is true both in experiments and in cases of spontaneous ESP: as many as 50 per cent of the latter occur when subjects are asleep or on the verge of sleep. The second is more subtle: the evidence is now very strong that ESP is most likely to occur when something odd happens: an unaccountable stray idea; a mistake in doing something; when something is done or said which is out of the ordinary.

How is this true in spontaneous ESP? Here is an example: a woman dials a 'phone number, and it turns out to be a *wrong* number. On the other end was a woman struggling to use the 'phone, who needed medical attention. The caller was able to get the number and summon help. A very useful 'mistake'.

In experimental ESP, this principle is most easily applied to picture-guessing ESP experiments. When subjects have impressions which seem odd – the kind of thing they would not have expected to think of – this often reflects ESP at work. So, some of the exercises here are designed to stimulate unfamiliar ways of thinking; loosening the constraints on thinking, getting out of habitual, stereotyped mental ruts.

Relaxing
It's a good idea to prepare for an ESP test as a subject by doing some brief relaxation exercises to get into the right state. For those who already practise yoga or meditation of some kind, fine. If not, *progressive relaxation* is a sound method.

Progressive relaxation
Take different areas of the body, concentrate on them one at a time, and alternately tense the muscles and then relax them, so that the relaxation is felt more deeply. Obviously this is *not* suitable if muscle tensing is painful for some reason – in those suffering from arthritis, for example. For most people it is a rapid way of getting very relaxed.

Sit in a comfortable chair, and don't wear tight or restrictive clothing; kick off your shoes. Now begin.

First, feet: tense the muscles in your feet *tight* and count slowly to five – 1, 2, 3, 4, 5. Now release all that tension suddenly and relax completely for another count of five. This tensing followed by sudden relaxation is the basis of the method and is performed twice for each part of the body. Start with the feet, followed by calves and then thighs. At this point, you must tense the entire limb for a count of ten and then relax *slowly*, breathing out as you do so.

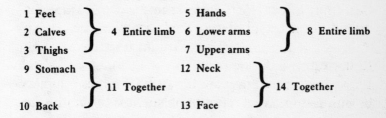

Finally, tense *all* the muscles in your body, and take in a good deep breath: hold that tension for a count of five; now relax, during a slow count of five, exhaling slowly. Your body should feel relaxed all over.

It is the contrast between tension and relaxation which generates deeper relaxation than other exercises and also increases your awareness and enjoyment of that relaxation. After you have tried the PR exercises a few times you may care to increase the number of cycles of tension/relaxation from two to three, and to go on holding the tension in the tension stage of the cycles for a count of ten rather than five. This will certainly increase the depth of relaxation you finally reach, but is best tried after you have done a few less lengthy sessions.

Relaxation exercises can be used in various ways: one

can use them just before trying an ESP test or game to get into the right mood and frame of mind; this can be done for card tests, picture-guessing tests, any type of ESP test.

Other methods

If you find that PR exercises are not suitable for some reason, or if you don't enjoy them, try yoga or meditation. But other, simpler methods are available. Try sitting in a comfortable chair, without restrictive or tight clothing, in a darkened or dimly lit room, and think about just one thing: a simple shape, a circle or a cross. Focus attention on that; shut out distracting images and impressions. Become more aware of your body relaxing – breath slowly and deeply – the tension dissipating from your muscles. This takes a little practice; at first you'll get distracted easily but it's worth persevering. Try to do any kind of relaxation exercise at a time when you know you'll have a good 15 or 20 minutes to yourself, when you feel at least in a neutral mood, and when you know you'll be free from distractions. Take the 'phone off the hook!

The American psychic Mary Craig Sinclair wrote about the ESP-favourable state she used in ESP testing:

The first thing you have to do is to learn the trick of undivided attention, or concentration ... The kind of concentration I mean is putting the attention on one object, or one *uncomplicated* thought, such as joy, or peace, and holding it there steadily. It isn't thinking; it is inhibiting thought, except for one thought, or one object in thought...Simultaneously (the person) must learn to relax, for, strangely enough, a part of concentration is complete relaxation.

Undivided concentration, then, means, for purposes of this experiment, a state of complete relaxation, under specified control. To concentrate in this undivided way you must first give yourself a "suggestion" to the effect that you will relax your mind and your body ... (from *Mental Radio* by Upton Sinclair)*.

Try practising some kind of relaxation exercise at least once a day, if you can, for a couple of weeks, to find for yourself the best way of getting relaxed. In addition to possibly increasing psi ability, regular relaxation exercises may very well improve general health.

Mental loosening up

Here are some entertaining exercises which stimulate creativity and 'lateral thinking'. The purpose of the exercises is to get you out of mental ruts; they are *not* tests of intelligence or logic, though some of them encourage you to solve puzzles in creative ways. Because the exercises involve playing around with ideas and words and language, they tend to combine well with free-response ESP tests (see Chapters 5, 6 and 7), where a similar flexibility and potential for creative imaginings exists.

There is indeed evidence that highly creative people do better at ESP tasks than less creative people, and

* Published by Werner Laurie, 1930; US revised second edition C. C. Thomas, 1962.

also that unusual ideas, images and impressions are particularly likely to involve ESP in free-response tests.

Exercise 1: Describing

Given a particular thing or object, how many adjectives can you think of to describe it in one minute (use a watch)? Each descriptive label should be a *single word*.

Here's an example: one person given a creativity test in which this describing game is used as a subtest was asked to think of words to describe a mountain stream, and came up with: clear, fresh, unpolluted, sparkling, gurgling, babbling, singing, shallow, rocky, cold, beautiful.

Here are some further words which can be used in this exercise: what adjectives can you think of in one minute to describe each of the following?:

A new Rolls-Royce	A village church
A supermarket	The Rolling Stones
The Tower of London	Valentine's Day cards
A tennis match	Space travel
A town crier	Hypnosis
A mountain	A ballet dancer
An aeroplane pilot	A magician
Nuclear weapons	Smoking cigarettes
Tigers	A rubbish dump
Newspapers	A doctor

There are no right and wrong answers to this game; but all the describing words must be adjectives. The aim is to stimulate a flow of ideas, as opposed to habit-pattern thinking – which is unfavourable to ESP. You can avoid it by choosing target words which are fairly concrete, rather than abstract nouns or nouns pertaining to emotional subjects. However, you will find that you cannot eliminate all habitual patterns of thought: certain kinds of adjectives tend to crop up more frequently than others, regardless of the trigger words used. At this stage, it is sufficient to be aware of them (make a note of them, and see Chapter 9 for a full discussion of their relevance).

If you are planning a telepathy experiment, it may be instructive for the subject and sender to try this exercise for the same three or four words each and to compare notes. Common sense suggests that subject/sender pairs may score better if their patterns of description are similar – if they're thinking in the same ways. Turn to Chapter 9 for more on this under-researched topic.

Exercise 2: Avoiding labels

In picture-guessing tests, several researchers have noted that subjects often tend to pick up a shape, or form, correctly and then mis-describe it by forcing some label on it from memory. Thus, a subject might see a brown spherical object and say 'I see a basketball', or a brown rectangular shape and say 'I see a door'. In fact they see brown spheres and rectangles, but they stick on a familiar label to make the image more familiar and easily categorized. ESP is not so familiar, and it isn't easily categorized. This tendency to label may lead to interference in picking up any ESP 'signals'. The first part of this exercise forces you to avoid convenient labels and makes you search for other ways of expressing yourself.

This game involves a speaker talking about some subject for one minute without using a key word or label. A questioner is allowed to butt in and ask questions, to try and make the speaker use the label they're avoiding.

Here are some examples:

1 Talk about football or tennis for one minute without using the word ball
2 Talk about the police for one minute without using the word crime
3 Talk about the weather for one minute without using the word rain
4 Talk about watching television for one minute without mentioning the name of particular programmes

The task is more difficult if you think of some topic where one word or label is used all the time.

The second part of the game involves pejorative labels, which are widely used and tend to inhibit thought. Try playing the role of someone, or represent some point of view, which is strongly labelled or disliked. Take the role of a peaceful Russian or a Third World dictator arguing against democracy. Try arguing for some cause you don't believe in or even feel is unpleasant or objectionable; the aim is to replace neat, black and white labelling ('Russians are warlike but Western democracy is wonderful') with some flexible thinking.

This may seem distant from ESP testing but this example shows that it isn't. In one picture-guessing ESP test we know of, a subject had as his target picture a photograph of a black man in prison in the United States, holding on to the prison bars and grimacing at the photographer (our view would be that such pictures should perhaps not be used; they are too emotive and negative in content, but not everyone would agree with that view). The subject reported several images of a grimacing and hostile black *ape*. In the judging, the subject placed this picture last – that is, as having the poorest correspondence with the target. Later, he admitted that he thought this picture almost certainly *was* the target, but he was afraid to place it first in the judging lest the experimenter considered him a racist. Such labels are very powerful.

Exercise 3: Uses

A game or exercise which features in many creativity tests is *uses*: given an object, what uses can be thought of for it? Thus a milk bottle can be used for containing milk or turpentine, or water; it can also be used for holding firework rockets, making abstract sculptures, Molotov cocktails, as a musical instrument, a weapon, a drinking vessel, a weight, and so on. Similar to the descriptions test, how many uses can you think of for each of the following in one minute?

Tin can	Sheet of paper
Plank of wood	Pillow
LP record	Cassette tape
Flowerpot	Bottle of ink
Rope	Pair of headphones
Cotton wool	Air freshener
Bar of soap	Telephone directory
Dartboard	Hair drier
Flagpole	Hatpin
Pack of cards	Fishing net

In another picture-test session a subject reported seeing a helicopter in the middle of a sea of candy floss and commented 'That's crazy, you don't get helicopters in the middle of candy floss'. The target indeed showed a helicopter in the middle of pink fluffy stuff which looked just like candy floss. Had he been more 'narrow minded', the subject may have missed a vital clue.

A variant on this theme is the combined object uses game. Pair off two objects which normally don't go together. What could these pairs be used for?:

A wire coathanger and a ball of string
A handkerchief and a shoelace
A newspaper and a metal rod
A safety pin and a rubber band
A pencil and a paper plate

Try to think of several uses for each combination; add your own ideas to those listed above.

Role playing: Alternatively, try imagining that you are someone else: what uses would a politician or a criminal have for bottles of ink, bars of soap, packs of cards? Although there is some risk of running into habit pattern thinking here (criminals could use soap bars to make chasing policemen slip up on pavements) the role-playing element is fun and again makes you think in someone else's shoes.

Left and right brains and psi

In recent years, psychologists have accumulated evidence to show that there are divisions of labour between the two halves of the human brain: the left and right *cerebral hemispheres*, together the cerebrum – much more highly developed in man than in any other creature. It is as if we had within ourselves two quite different selves; and there is evidence of some

Left	Right
	Psi?
	Fantasy
Language	Dance
Writing	Perception
Mathematics	Art and music appreciation

antagonism between the two types of functioning – left hemisphere dominant and right hemisphere dominant (or L mode and R mode as they have been termed). In the large majority of individuals the left hemisphere dominates.

Which mode for psi ability?

What has this to do with psi aptitude? It seems likely that L-mode activity is logical, analytical and precise, while R-mode activity is spatial, metaphorical, emotional and 'irrational'. Then perhaps R-mode activity is more favourable for psi than L-mode activity.

Mode stimulators

William Braud, at the University of Houston, Texas, has used R-mode stimulating conditions and found them to produce significantly better psi than L-mode stimulators. Some of the following exercises are derived from these R-mode stimulators.

Exercise 4: Imagery

These follow on naturally from relaxation exercises, and are preparation for picture-guessing ESP experiments. Carry out these exercises sometime when you know you won't be disturbed, and somewhere quiet. Relax in a comfortable chair and begin to clear your mind of any thoughts. Close your eyes and imagine a simple black horizontal line running across from right to left; just 'watch' that line in your mind's eye. This stills distracting mental activity.

Sensations: Try to conjure up feelings and images of some scene or state – a sensation, such as cold, is a good starting point. Can you imagine that your skin is cold? 'See' in your mind's eye, if you can, a snowy plain; icebergs in the sea; or just falling snow. Try to avoid labels at this stage.

Different individuals have very different visual (and other) imagery abilities. If you don't visualize easily, don't persist with the exercise; but try it a few times first though!

Imaging scenes: If you do find imaging easy and comfortable, try slightly more complex things. Start with a single theme – the sea, or jungles, or New York. Can you 'hear' things as well as 'see' them? Can you hear the traffic in streets in New York? Can you also make things happen? Can you make birds fly in the direction you want them to, make images change colour?

Using the exercises

The various exercises suggested in this chapter have several different uses. First, they're actually enjoyable and fun, especially the mental loosening-up exercises played in groups. The imaging and drawing exercises may develop latent visual-spatial abilities.

Second, the exercises can be done just before psi tests to get into the right mood, as preparations. It is, of course, possible to carry out tests with and without such preparations, to see if the exercises really *do* stimulate psi; and it may be that longer term use of the exercises permanently improves psi ability. Both of these topics are discussed further in Chapter 9.

The golden rule about all the exercises is: if you don't find them enjoyable or interesting, don't bother with them. It is certainly true that exercises which some people find enjoyable, others find tedious; and you can't expect everyone to enjoy all the exercises. Do them only if they're fun!

4

Simple Psi Games: Cards and Dice

The games in this chapter are designed to be simple demonstrations of psi effects: in the card games you will be trying to guess a predetermined sequence, either from the cards or via a sender (mind-to-matter and mind-to-mind ESP); in the dice tests you will be trying to influence how the dice fall (mind-over-matter, or PK). We explain various methods of assessing the results, whether individual scores, differences between scores or combined scores.

ESP card tests

It was J. B. Rhine's card tests, performed at Duke University, North Carolina, that first brought parapsychology to the attention of the academic world in the 1930s. He used special five-card packs of cards—25 cards in each, five cards of each kind (he devised special symbols). With these, he demonstrated a simple test for measuring the possible influence of psi. The subject endeavoured to guess the sequence of cards in a well-shuffled pack. As we explained in Chapter 2, because Rhine knew the probability of any one of the five types occupying a particular place in the sequence, he was able to say whether the scores were determined by anything other than chance.

Our card games are simple versions of Rhine's tests, using ordinary playing cards. You can play them on your own or in groups of two or more people. The scoring is explained after each game, but *remember*, these games are a prelude to the later, more rigid experiments described in Chapters 5, 6 and 7; they do not provide unequivocal evidence of psi. Try them and enjoy them.

For all these tests you will need an ordinary pack of playing cards with the jokers removed, a pen and some paper.

GAME 1: SIMPLE CLAIRVOYANCE

Do not look at the card faces until it is time to score. Try this 5, 10, 20 or 50 times.

1 Shuffle the pack.

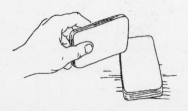

2 Lift off the top ten cards and put the other 42 out of the way.

3 Using these ten cards, try to guess the colour on the face of the top card. If you think it is a red card, put it in a pile to your right; if black, in a pile to your left. (Remember: <u>R</u>ed to your <u>R</u>ight.) Repeat this for the remaining nine cards.

4 When you have finished, turn the cards over so that you can see their faces, leaving them in two piles – left and right. The number correct out of ten is the number of red cards in the right-hand pile plus the number of black cards in the left-hand pile. Make a note of the score.

5 Put the ten cards back in the main pack, reshuffle and repeat the test the required number of times.

Score card: 1 in 2 individual score

Total number of guesses _____
Number of hits_____

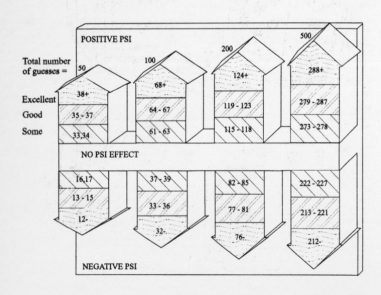

Find your score.

Example: If your number of guesses is 100, and you score 65 hits then you show *good* psi ability.

GAME 2: MOVING TO TEAMWORK

To introduce a competitive element, two people can take the test together. As before, do not look at the faces until it is time. Do this 5, 10, 20 or 50 times each.

1 Shuffle the pack.

2 Each player takes ten cards each off the top (put the other 32 out of the way).

3 Take turns to guess the colour of the top card of your packs, and check the results each time.

4 When you have finished, check the piles again.

5 This method can be extended to four players, or you could have two teams of two players each (each team making a total of 20 guesses).

Scoring in groups: Counting up the scores player by player, one card at a time, can be quite exciting; and with the competitive testing, there are two factors which are interesting. The first is whether either or both of the teams or players have scored significantly above or below chance. Use the score key given for Game 1.

The other question is whether there is a significant *difference between* the scores of the two players/teams, which would also suggest the possible operation of ESP. Our second score key will tell you. This normally means that one player/team has more psiability than the other, but that neither shows a strong enough psi effect on their own.

Score card: 1 in 2 significant differences

Total number of guesses _____

Scores
    Player 1 _____
    Player 2 _____
    Difference_____

Find your score.

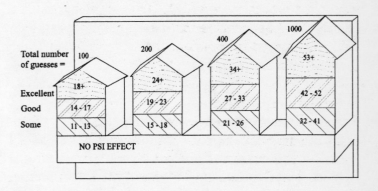

Thus, one can get *individual scores* which will be significantly above, or below, chance. Also, with a competitive test involving two teams or players, we might also
get a *significant difference between players.*

GAME 3: SIMPLE TELEPATHY

You will need another person to act as sender. The
sender sits with the cards at a table, not facing the

subject—who should sit comfortably. This avoids the possibility of the sender unwittingly giving clues to the subject. Try this 5, 10, 20 or 50 times.

1 Sender shuffles the pack.
2 Sender takes ten cards from the top of the pack and says 'Ready' when this is done.

3 Sender turns over the top card and looks at the face. Subject makes his guess. If he guesses red, the sender places the card to his right (<u>R</u>ed to <u>R</u>ight); black, to his left. This is done regardless of what the card is.
4 Repeat for the remaining nine cards. Sender then says 'Finished'.
5 Score for correct guesses as before.
6 Repeat test.

To evaluate the results, use the score key on p.62.

Two things may need practice here. The first is that if the subject tends to guess really quickly the sender may just not be able to keep up! Practice will tend to smooth this over, a rhythm is easy to get into. If the problem persists, the sender can use some signal to tell the subject when he's turned over the next card; a tap of the pen on the table perhaps.

The other problem is more tricky. The sender may tend to make a particular error which will falsely inflate the score. He may tend to put to his right cards which have red faces rather than those which the subject actually *guessed* red, and similarly put black-faced cards to his left rather than those the subject guessed were black. This error is very easily made and cannot be detected after the event. It may help to put two index cards or postcards on the left and right of the desk or table top, clearly labelled 'guessed red' and 'guessed black', to act as prompts.

This type of test leads naturally to teamwork – the two people may well wish to alternate the roles of subject and sender. Under these conditions it is quite likely that the outcome will be a significant score when the two individual subject scores are added together, unless it is the case that one person very strongly prefers the role of sender while the other strongly prefers the role of subject. Here one might expect a significant difference between the two!

More sensitive tests

Using the 1 in 2 test (guessing red or black with cards) is not a very sensitive way of testing for ESP, but it is simple and fast. A more sensitive measure is to try guessing the *suits* of the cards (hearts, clubs, diamonds, spades) rather than just the colours alone. Now we are using a 1 in 4 test method.

1 in 4 test: Modifying the test procedures given in the previous pages should be easy: you simply put cards in four piles rather than two. It is a good idea to use a postcard or index card with the appropriate symbol drawn on it to mark each pile. It is annoying to forget halfway through which pile consists of the cards you think are spades!

Score card: 1 in 4 individual scores

   Total number of guesses _____

Number of hits _____

(See below for score key.)

1 in 10 test: Trying to guess the *number*, or value, of cards is possibly not a good idea. One has here a 1 in 13 test: not an easy value to play around with. The best bet would be to exclude the face cards (king, queen, jack), leaving a 1 in 10 test using aces as ones. Table IV is provided for such 1 in 10 tests. Certainly the 1 in 10 test is a sensitive one; but there are drawbacks and therefore we do not recommend it. First, one needs ten separate piles of cards. Second, each individual test has to

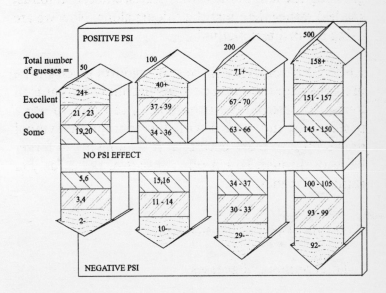

be extended beyond ten trials: probably at least 25 trials per test. A small number of trials per test tends to make for short, snappy, episodes: long tests can produce declining scores. And with 1 in 10 tests, the individual tests will need to be moderately lengthy, since the statistics applied to ESP test data become complex with low-chance probabilities like 1 in 10 and small numbers of guesses. However, if you want to try, Table IV is there: some subjects have told us that with card guessing they feel an affinity towards numbers rather than colours or suits.

Score card: 1 in 10 individual scores
   Procedure: Use game 1, but guess for numbers.

   Number of guesses_____
   Number of hits_____

NB For 1 in 10 tests there are no negative values.

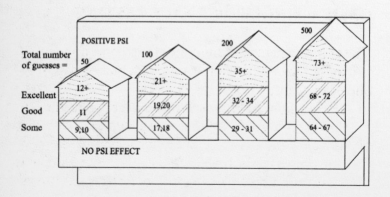

Dice PK tests

The PK tests we describe are not that different from the original dice tests developed by none other than J.B. Rhine. The idea started from an interest in gambling, and he then went on to spend many years performing experiments before he published any of the results, refining techniques and eliminating possible sources of error. Although we do not have access to complicated pieces of equipment it is very easy to perform simple, accurate tests, in fact, more so than simple ESP tests. The central problem with using dice for testing PK is that commercially available dice are rather biased. There is a definite tendency for the high faces to come up more often than the low faces, since the high faces are lighter, having more material scooped out of them. The two basic tests we suggest get round this problem. For all these tests you will need one or more six-sided dice, a small plastic cup or container and a pen and some paper.

GAME 4: SINGLE DICE FACE TESTING

The aim is to make different dice faces come up in turn, to avoid the possibility of introducing bias by choosing one or two faces.

1 Decide how many tests you are going to do (36 throws is a good number – aim for each face six times). Take the faces in any order but be sure to aim properly six times for each face. Write down what your aim is going to be for the first six throws

and start. To get accurate results you must keep careful records. Step 5 shows how.

2 Shake the dice around in the cup and throw it at a hard surface (a wall is ideal; a tabletop is suitable). When the dice comes to rest, record the face shown under the 'Aim' heading. Repeat five times for that target face. Each time you record a face, have another look to make sure.

3 Repeat the procedure for each target face until all 36 throws have been made.

4 Record the number of hits.

5 The finished table of results should look like this. You should check that you have six figures in each column.

Score card: 1 in 6

Aim 1	Aim 2	Aim 3	Aim 4	Aim 5	Aim 6
_____	_____	_____	_____	_____	_____
_____	_____	_____	_____	_____	_____
_____	_____	_____	_____	_____	_____
_____	_____	_____	_____	_____	_____
_____	_____	_____	_____	_____	_____
_____	_____	_____	_____	_____	_____

Hits:

_____ _____ _____ _____ _____ _____ Total _____

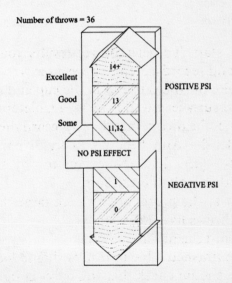

Number of throws = 36

Competition in PK

There seems psychologically to be something about PK tests which naturally suggests the possibility of competitive testing. The laboratory evidence on competitive PK testing is sparse and more evidence is needed: an area for exploration! Here are two competitive games to play.

GAME 5: INTRODUCING COMPETITION

This is a variation of Game 4, for two players.

1 Each player throws the dice 36 times, aiming for each face six times.
2 Player A starts aiming for one face and makes his six throws. Both players together can record the dice face after each throw (this minimizes errors).
3 Player B makes his six throws for the same face; again both players record the scores.
4 Repeat the procedure for each face in turn.

Score card: Competitive PK 1 in 6 test.

Total number of throws _____
Scores
    Player 1_____
    Player 2_____
    Difference_____

Total number of throws = 72

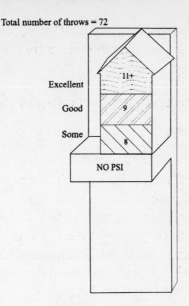

Excellent — 11+

Good — 9

Some — 8

NO PSI

GAME 6: AIMING HIGH AND LOW

Another competitive game for two players.

1 Player A throws ten times, aiming high – 4, 5 or 6 is a hit; 1, 2 or 3 is a miss. Scores are again recorded by both players.

2 Player B then throws ten times aiming high, scoring as before.

3 Both players then take it in turns to throw ten times, aiming low. In this case, the scoring is reversed – 1, 2 or 3 is a hit; 4, 5 or 6 is a miss.

4 Each player makes 20 throws each.

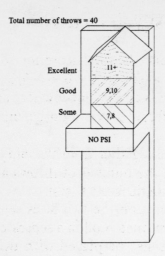

Total number of throws = 40

Excellent — 11+
Good — 9,10
Some — 7,8
NO PSI

Score card: Competitive PK 1 in 2 test.

Total number of throws _____
Number of hits_____

The sevens test for PK

This test represents another neat way of solving dice bias in PK tests. The difference from the PK testing in Game 4 is that you will need *two* dice for this test.

Again, individual player/team scores may be significant, there may be a significant difference between player/team scores; or the combined score of players/teams may be significant.

GAME 7: THE 'SEVENS' TEST

The aim is to make the total score for two dice faces together come up as seven: 1 + 6, 2 + 5, 3 + 4, 4 + 3, 5 + 2, 6 + 1. There is always one low face and one high face so that the effect of bias is almost completely eliminated.

1 Throw the dice together from the cup. There is no need to make the number of throws a multiple of six, as in the single face PK test.

2 Record the scores on the two faces separately, and record the combined total in a separate column.

3 This game can also be played with two players or teams of players. Decide on a fixed number of throws – 25 or 50 say – and see who can score the most sevens.

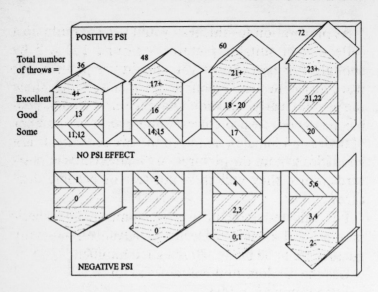

Score card: Individual sevens PK test 1 in 6

Number of throws _____
Number of 'sevens' _____

To score for significant differences use the key on p.64, inserting your numbers of 'sevens' under 'scores'.

An ESP test with people as targets
This is a simple 1 in 2 test using pictures of people as targets. It's similar to the test used with the Psi Star Lalsingh Harribance (see Introduction); the basic test is to guess the sex of people shown in concealed pictures.

As preparation for this test, you'll need to build up a collection of suitable pictures – around 100 will be enough. For best results you should use pictures cut from magazines and colour supplements, which show the people clearly. You don't have to select famous people, just good, clear pictures. Choose an equal number of males and females, and keep the two separate. It is a good idea to gum the pictures on to index cards or postcards, since they will then not tear or become dogeared.

For this test, you need a randomizer, an experimenter, and a subject. Decide in advance how many guesses are to be made –20 is a good number.

Use the random-number tables as follows:

Even numbers = Male

Odd numbers = Female

GAME 8: PICTURE TEST

1 The randomizer prepares the sequence of 20 targets, keeping a record of the order.
2 Each picture is placed inside two envelopes.
   Number targets from 1 to 20 on the outside

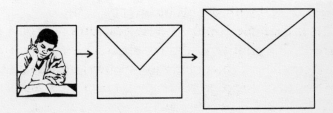

envelopes. You should seal the outer envelopes, even if not the inner ones.

3 Randomizer passes envelopes to experimenter.

4 The experimenter hands the envelopes one by one to the subject who guesses the sex of the people in the pictures, taking as much time as necessary. The experimenter then writes down any impressions that the subject may have.

5 When the guesses are complete, the experimenter and subject go through the photos and score the results.

There is no statistical reason to write down the subject's impressions, but you may find some amusing results. For example, Carl Sargent recalls a subject describing a target as 'female, a very sensitive person – maybe artistic; a sense of refinement, and a liberal and humanitarian outlook'. The concealed picture was of Ronald Reagan!

Score your results using the 1 in 2 key on p. 62 or Table I.

Using the simple tests

The tests outlined here are simple, but they are important in two particular ways. First, playing with these simple games and tests will get you used to recording and checking results.

The second thing about these simple tests is that they will act as a stepping stone. Almost everyone will find interesting things going on in a series of tests. Perhaps

you will have a strong hunch that things are really going well – and you get a very high score. Or maybe you
find that you score better in the evening than at
lunchtime, or that of your three children, one seems to
score much better than the other two. If you play the
games with friends, you may find that those people who
score high in one type of test, score high in others too.
If you want to look at test-score differences, then you'll
need to check out some of the more sophisticated tests
and experiments outlined later (pp. 83–160). So you
must feel happy first about the simpler tests we've been
through so far.

5

Picture Testing for ESP

Free-response tests
If a subject in a telepathy experiment tries to pick up something about a picture which a sender is seeing – a picture showing a reasonably complex, detailed scene with definite form and content – he is *not* reduced to deciding between one of a handful of possibilities as in forced-choice tests. For this reason picture tests are often called *free-response* tests. There is a flexibility about free-response tests which forced-choice tests lack.

Measurement: With simple card guessing, there is no problem of measurement, as we have seen. If one guesses 'red' for a card and it is the seven of hearts, that is correct. But if a sender is looking at a picture of Concorde, and the subject 'sees' a flock of swans in flight, is this correct? Many people might think so: seeing large white birds flying is not a perfect hit (the subject didn't actually see Concorde), but good enough. Most people would probably score a 'hit'. A sceptic, however, might argue that the subject was wrong: he didn't see an aeroplane.

But what if the subject sees a flight of ducks, *not* white birds? Or a large oil tanker standing on a runway (which could be waiting to refuel Concorde)? Some might score a 'hit', thinking the subject was generally on the right track; others would disagree. This problem of *scoring being subjective* is basic to free-response tests and the methods for overcoming are explained later (see p. 95).

What are the odds against chance?

There is a second problem. Even in the rare cases where everyone could agree that a hit has been scored, what are the odds against chance being involved? One subject, in a telepathy experiment run by Sargent, had as his target picture William Blake's painting 'The Ancient of Days', and reported 'Oh, it's that picture by Blake of God with the dividers creating the world'. There is no doubt that this is a hit. But what are the odds against chance? A hundred to one or several million to one? The subject may have known that the experimenters were partial to Blake's paintings, but there is no way he could have worked out that this picture would be the target, chosen from a pool of several hundred pictures. To help us to work out an odds-against-chance figure, we must change the test procedure.

How to measure chance

We *have* to introduce a forced-choice component some-where along the line. This is done by selecting a limited number (usually four) of diverse pictures – a guessing set – one of which is a copy of the target. After the subject has made his guess about what the target pic-ture may show, he is shown the four pictures and he is asked to choose between them. If he picks out the 'right' one (the target copy), the chance probability for doing this is 1 in 4. The subject's judgements still con-tain a subjective element; but our final measure is ob-jective and we can evaluate the subject's performance.

Reducing errors

There are two important elements here to be noted. First, we must use a *copy* of the target. If we used the original (in a telepathy test, the one the sender had been looking at), we may be providing sensory cues: the sen-der may have handled the target picture more and left more fingerprints. Second, the pictures we use for our sets should be very different one from another, or else the subject may become confused when making his judgement. We explain how this is done on pp. 90–93.

Basic telepathic picture testing

For this test, you need three people: an experimenter, a subject and a sender. You also need duplicate copies of a set of pictures, which the experimenter should pre-pare beforehand.

Finally, you will need to use two rooms in this

'experiment; there should be no way of seeing or hearing in one room anything that occurs in the other. The sender and experimenter should both have paper and pens.

Preparing pictures

One set of the four pictures (1, 2, 3 and 4) should be individually sealed in correspondingly numbered envelopes, so that each envelope contains only one picture. (You may use adhesive labels to number them.) This is the 'sending set'.

The *duplicate set* of those four pictures should be numbered in the same way as the first. This set can be contained in a single large envelope: label this on the front as 'judging set'.

The sender has the guessing set in room 2; the experimenter has the *judging set* in room 1.

Choosing the target

This is done by the sender, during the experiment as he sits in room 2. For this you will need to use Table V (Appendix 1, p.189). Close your eyes and put the tip of your finger on to the page. Open your eyes and put the tip of your finger on to the page. Open your eyes. Your finger will be pointing to a number in the table of random digits (0–9). Find your target from the following:

Number 1 or 5   Target is picture 1
Number 2 or 6   Target is picture 2

Number 3 or 7	Target is picture 3
Number 4 or 8	Target is picture 4
Number 9 or 0	Ignore this digit and read on to the next one

As an example, let's say we found our finger was pointing like this:

54418 57390 01662

Ignore the zero and read on. Another zero! Ignore that too. The next number is a 1 – so picture 1 is the target. Take envelope 1 and open it carefully.

Mental preparation

As the subject and sender are both attempting to communicate using psi ability (or so we hope), it follows that it will help the subject and maybe the sender also to prepare by using the progressive relaxation technique described in Chapter 3. It will also help the subject if a low level of lighting is used in room 1. As he speaks his thoughts (impressions, feelings, visual images) he should try to mention everything, however irrelevant it may seem. The sender should, meanwhile, be studying the target picture. Look at it – study its theme and form. Then look at details; try sketching bits of it. Most important, concentrate.

EXPERIMENT 1: BASIC TELEPATHIC PICTURE TESTING

1 The subject settles comfortably in room 1, in the presence of the sender and experimenter.
2 The sender leaves when the subject feels ready to

begin, and goes to room 2. The experimenter begins timing.

3 The subject lets his thoughts drift and speaks them out loud. (Not too loud: this could upset relaxation.) The experimenter writes them down.
4 The sender settles in room 2 and selects the target picture (see Preparation). He then concentrates on it, taking note of its form and content.
5 When the experimenter has timed 15 minutes, he ends the experiment, notifying the sender, who remains in room 2.

6 The experimenter and subject assess the judging
   set and rank the pictures in the order of their likelihood of being the target picture. Keep a perma-
   nent record, like this:

Date: 15 Feb 1996
Subject: Brian Jones
Sender: Peter Smith
First choice: Picture 3
Second choice: Picture 1
Third choice: Picture 4
Fourth choice: Picture 2

7 The experimenter then calls in the sender who can
  tell everyone what the target is:

The target was: Picture three
    which was

First choice. Direct hit.

This is the *basic* test procedure. There are three features
which need some more detailing: choosing which pictures to use, how to go about the judging and evaluating
the results.

Choosing pictures
You are probably going to need several *different* sets of
pictures if you want to test the same subject several
times: if you re-use the same pictures over and over

again, subjects will start to try guessing which picture is the target. 'I see a brown rectangle…so maybe that's the door in the picture with Christ in it'. In this case, rational thinking is being substituted for real receptivity, and this tends to inhibit ESP.

What to look for

Try and choose pictures which have a clear content and some obvious meaning. They should be moderately detailed – not too bare and not too fussy. Avoid pictures which are surrealistic, or ones which show several different things. Also, avoid pictures which show very unpleasant scenes (like war atrocities) since experimental evidence suggests that these don't make good targets: go for pictures which you find attractive. One researcher suggested that a really good picture is one which you would stop and look at if it was in a Sunday newspaper colour magazine, which is not a bad criterion to use. Collect a variety of subjects too: sporting pictures (with colour and movement these can make good targets), nature scenes with dramatic scenery, humorous pictures, science-fiction or fantasy pictures and so on.

If the picture is on thin paper, or has some other scene on the back, this may be confusing or distracting for the participants. Glue them to stiff pieces of card: this strengthens flimsy pictures and obscures anything on the reverse.

Making up sets

For making up a set of four, you must choose four very different pictures. For each of the two copies of the set, make sure that each picture is clearly labelled on the back, and that the labels correspond. If you make up several sets, label the sets 'set A', 'set B' and so on; within each individual set label the pictures 'A1, A2, A3, A4'; 'B1, B2, B3, B4' and so on. Keep the pictures in clearly marked envelopes as instructed above (see basic test procedure).

You can, of course, keep expanding your picture collection. Carl Sargent started by using just eight sets of pictures in picture-guessing tests, and after four years now has no less than 88. Don't worry, though, six to ten sets is enough to begin with!

For choosing a set from your collection for use in a session use the random numbers on pp. 189–191. If you have 10 sets of pictures or fewer, simply select one random number (for zero, read 10). If you have more than 10 sets, read off two digits at a time. Thus, in the example shown earlier, '00' would be set 100 (you're unlikely to have that many sets, so ignore this and read on), '16' would be set 16, and so on. But do make sure that you don't select for use a set which the subject and sender have seen before. Here again one can see the importance of keeping a record of all the sessions you do.

Judging

Judging is an acquired skill. Do it properly because the success of the experiment hangs on it. Make sure you

follow these instructions.
1 Don't rush.
2 Look at all the pictures – even though you are sure
   you know the target!
3 Compare notes with each picture in turn.
4 Award a score using the following:

0 points:	no match between idea/image and picture
1,2 points:	a minor correspondence
3,4 points:	a fair correspondence, or a good correspondence for an idea or image which is not unusual, e.g. a tree, a boat, a bird
5,6 points:	a good correspondence, with some detail
7,8 points:	a strong correspondence, with something slightly unusual about it, or some extra correct detail
9 points:	a really strong correspondence, almost perfect, with good detail
10 points:	absolutely spot-on, with good detail, an excellent match.

Factors determining your choice

1 *Basic shapes* Did a particular shape dominate your
   impressions – circles, rectangles, triangles? Look
   for a picture (or pictures) likewise dominated.
2 *Colours* Did any particular colours dominate your
   impressions, and, if so, do any pictures show these

colours strongly? Or did you get no impressions of colours at all – in this case look for black-and-white or monochrome pictures.

3 *Movement* Did your impressions seem mainly of active, moving elements or static, 'freeze-frame' elements?

4 *Emotion and mood* Did you experience a strong mood or emotion – humour, quietness, tranquillity, sadness? The stronger the match between the impression and the picture(s), the higher the score on the 0–10 point scale we suggest. If, for example, you once or twice 'saw' green and one picture has some green in it, a low score (1 or 2 points). If you were struck by a strong impression of green, or 'saw' it frequently, and a picture shows green very prominently, a higher score (around 5 points).

5 *Detail* There are literally thousands of possible contents for impressions and pictures. You may wish, perhaps, to think in terms of looking for correspondences in certain basic categories first. Examples would be: people (presence or absence; then more detail – age, sex, and so on), animals, architectural details and buildings, 'nature' elements (water, plant life, skies, horizons and so on), religious or mystical elements (clearly this is going to overlap with mood and emotion components), machinery and implements (aircraft, cars, etc.), and so on.

The correspondences between pictures and images and impressions can be direct, or symbolic (flying birds as symbols of freedom), or simply emotional – a shared feeling. Some impressions may be more likely to be accurate than others, however, and in the next chapter we shall discuss how to separate the 'wheat' (accurate ESP) from the 'chaff' (distractions, errors, false alarms).

Problem of subjectivity

A concern that many people have about picture-guessing experiments is the feeling that, if one simply says lots and lots of different things, then something *must* match the target picture. But this doesn't invalidate the experiment because the various things said will – in the absence of ESP – be more or less equally divided in correspondences between all four pictures. Without some ESP, there is *no* way in which the target picture will score more points in judging than the others to a significant extent. Lots of impressions, in the absence of ESP, will simply be random noise.

As some measure of how serious a problem subjectivity is, one can use *two* judges to see how well they agree. After the experiment with subject and experimenter (and sender) is finished, give a copy of the subjects impressions, together with the four pictures used in judging, to an independent judge – someone who should know nothing of the outcome of the session, or what the target was. Ask the independent judge to score the results, using rank judgements, just as the subject did. Over a series of trials, see how often the subject and judge put the same picture first in their judging. If the judging is *totally* subjective, they will only agree 25 per cent of the time. If they agree significantly more often than 25 per cent of the time, then there clearly is not total subjectivity. You can evaluate the significance of the agreement rate just as you would for the significance of the direct hit rate on the targets.

With long sessions, where a subject gets a lot of impressions and ideas, this blow-by-blow scoring can be time-consuming. But it does help to make judging more reliable. It ensures that the subject takes all relevant images and impressions into account when making the judgements.

Scoring the results

There are two ways of scoring the results, one of which is fairly obvious: simply the significance of how many guesses in judging were correct. Here we just look at how many times the subject placed the target picture first in judging. The score key given on p.68 for individual 1 in 4 tests will tell you how well you have done.

Another way of scoring is not so obvious but it is more sensitive. ESP is not always capable of giving full information about things – like when someone simply *knows* that they must go home, but they don't know why. Perhaps, in picture tests, people might sometimes pick up a little bit of information about the target but not quite enough to place it first in judging.

Again, perhaps ESP sometimes might give *negative* –

say, 'there's nothing particularly funny or amusing about the target'. This may help you to pick the right, target, picture out of the other three (with our set, this negative information would tell you the target wasn't picture 3 – but not whether it was 1, 2 or 4).

A more sensitive measure of ESP is the *rank sum* method. The details are explained in Appendix 2 should you want to derive it for yourself. This time, the number you obtain (and look up on the key) is the rank sum of your results. You must do at least 25 tests to use this key, otherwise your results will not be valid.

To find your rank sum, add together the choices you made for the target in each test (first, second, third, etc.). A *chance* score would be the *average* times the number of choices and the average value per choice is $\frac{1}{4}(1+2+3+4) = 2.5$. So for a series of, say, five choices, the chance average rank sum would be 12.5 (i.e. 5×2.5). A *better than chance score* gives a *lower* value than the average; because a good score means a *low* number (choose right, a direct hit, gives a value of 1; *first* choice correct) and likewise a worse than chance score gives a higher value.

Score card: 1 in 4 individual rank sum test

Number of guesses _____
(must be greater than 25)
Rank sum of target answers _____

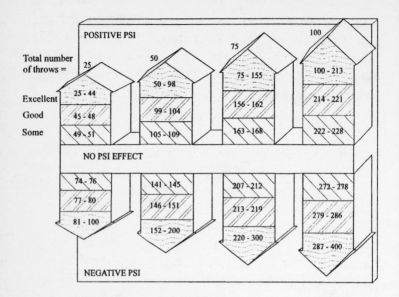

Two-person telepathy testing

It may well be that there is someone you know particularly well with whom you'd like to try this picture testing and you feel a third person would get in the way, or
maybe it just isn't convenient to have three people
around. The procedure for Experiment 1 can easily be
modified for two people: a sender and a subject-
experimenter. The subject sits alone and tries to get
impressions, either writing them down, or better still,
taping them and then doing the judging alone. But you
must use a third party to make up the picture sets so
that you don't know what they are.

Finally, there's a trade-off with picture tests: they
tend to give better results than forced-choice tests, but

they are fairly time-consuming. In a couple of hours you will only get through a handful of guesses. The following chapters will show you how to improve your results using techniques developed by researchers in the field.

6

Dream Psi

Dreams have long been associated with both telepathy and foretelling the future. Before the Great Sphinx in Egypt stands a tablet of stone, erected by order of Pharaoh Tutmes IV, recording a dream predicting a long and successful reign; and a more famous Pharaoh's dream (as interpreted by Joseph) is related in the Bible. In some cultures, people believe that dreams are caused by spirits of the dead, or by telepathy directly.

Careful research has shown that the dream state is indeed favourable for ESP, and in this chapter we aim to investigate this relationship. But first we should know something of the psychology of dreaming and how to stimulate dream recall. Many people do not recall their dreams well and often, but they can improve with training.

Dreaming and eye movements

Much of what psychologists now know of dreaming

derives from the discovery in the early 1950s of observable physiological changes when we dream. In 1953, Eugene Aserinsky and Nathaniel Kleitman reported that, at periodic intervals during the night, individuals show short bursts of rapid eye movement (REM)

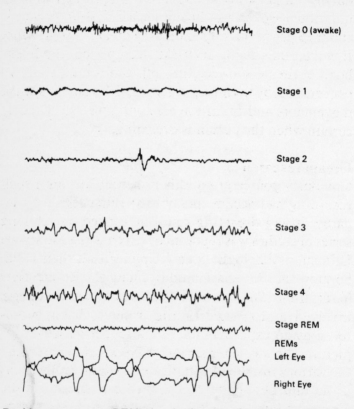

Rapid eye movement (REM) sleep begins only after the sleeper has passed through stages 1 to 4 of sleep. The top six traces show brain activity; the bottom two show the movement of the eyeballs during REM sleep, measured from left and right eyes.

activity: eye muscles move the eye as if the sleeper were scanning images. Brain-wave activity (recorded as an electroencephalogram, or EEC) is also different at this time from ordinary sleep. There are usually four to six such bursts of activity, lasting around 15–30 minutes during a night's sleep. The interesting thing is that an individual woken up during an REM sleep period is about 75 per cent likely to report a dream of some kind. If woken up outside an REM sleep period, the likelihood of the person recalling a dream is only about 10 per cent. So, by wiring up a sleeper with monitors of eye movements and brain-wave activity, we can be fairly certain when the person is dreaming.

Dream research
Obviously you can't try this at home! But once such recording had become possible, the first tests for telepathy during dreaming could be carried out. A long series of studies was reported by psychiatrist Montague Ullman, psychologist Stan Krippner, and their collaborators at the Maimonides Medical Center, New York, from 1960 onwards. Their basic test procedure involved a sleeping/dreaming receiver being monitored by an experimenter, and a sender with a target picture who was sent a signal by the experimenter when the various instruments indicated that the receiver was dreaming. The sender would then concentrate on the picture and try to affect the receiver's dreaming to conform with the content of the picture. The judging was basically the same as the procedure given for picture-

guessing tests (pp. 92–97), although outside judges with special knowledge of dream psychology were often used.

Over the years, these experiments provided very strong evidence of telepathic dreaming. Of 14 studies, half produced statistically significant evidence of telepathy, some of them showing very high scoring rates. With a chance 'hit rate' of 25 per cent, actual scoring rates for three of the best experiments were 75, 62.5 and 62.5 per cent (again). This is certainly ESP on the grand scale.

Recent experiments

There has been no serious attempt to replicate these findings. Other researchers have tried one-off or two-experiment follow-ups, but such small-scale efforts cannot compare with a decade of expensive and time-consuming research. In fact the one-off shots had some success; but in recent years, dream ESP researchers have turned away from the Maimonides approach because the experiments are so expensive to run, requiring insomniac experimenters and full sleep-laboratory facilities.

The emphasis is now on simplified versions. Attempts have been made to get dream recall from subjects when they wake up in the morning, and to use pre-sleep sending (the sender looks at the target picture just before going to sleep himself) or clairvoyance tests. In some Cambridge experiments on dream ESP, fluent dreamers were specially selected for the experiments, so that there was no need to get information about dreams during the night, since the subjects remembered much of their dreams the next day. Inevitably, some material will still be lost; the Maimonides approach was the best, but the waking-recall method is proving to be a reasonable alternative.

Keeping a dream diary

The first step with any experiment is to start a dream diary, where you record all dreams you recall from the night before. You may have difficulty at first in recalling much but the following ideas may help you.

It has often been reported that if people doze happily for some time after beginning to wake, their dream recall is much poorer than if they wake quickly. Dream material seems to be lost from conscious ability to recall it fairly soon after wakefulness sets in. So, when you're aware that you're no longer asleep, wake yourself fully, and see what you can recall of your dreams. You will find that, if you do this regularly, dream recall will improve.

If the prospect of losing precious dozing time is too unpleasant, there is an alternative. Try to wake enough to write down a few key words in your diary (or even speak them into a bedside cassette recorder) which may act as triggers for later, fuller, recall. Then you can go back to dozing!

The British dream ESP researcher Trevor Harley carries this one step further by periodically waking during the night and writing down such key words and phrases and then writing his dreams up in full later in the morning. If you tend naturally to wake occasionally during the night, this is not a bad idea.

You may also find that during the day you recall extra fragments of dreams from the previous night – something happens which triggers recall. Record these extra fragments in your dream diary too.

Analysing dreams

Free associations: While most dreams do mean something, their meaning is sometimes distorted or disguised. Free association helps to discover the underlying meaning of the dream and increases and deepens dream recall.

Often, fairly trivial events of the day before may be involved in the dreaming process as part of background scenery. Were those events really trivial, or did they relate to something important which may be reflected in the dream? If an element appears in a dream which seems to be completely meaningless, it's quite possible that it (the element) really *is* meaningless (a point Freud never grasped). Alternatively, what things spring to mind when you think of that element?

Here's an example of a small-scale dream element and its interpretation. One subject in a dream experiment reported a scene in which she was hitting a walrus with an oar, on a paisley-patterned beach. Odd, certainly; but she recalled that a couple of days before she had seen a walrus in a television documentary on wildlife, just after a disliked uncle had been visiting. Indeed, she mused, he did look somewhat like a walrus, being fat and having a horrid moustache. And on the floor of the living room in the uncle's house was – yes, a dreadful paisley-patterned carpet. Finally, the girl was broke at the time, and the uncle, rich and notoriously mean. Hence, probably, the hitting with an oar.

Dream analysis has spawned too many charlatans to be completely reputable – you should ignore Freudian books on dreams, and also the preposterous 'dream dictionaries' which tell you in all seriousness that if you dream of a zebra it means your nephew is going to get married. However, by using common sense one can often extract meaning from dreams which is only hidden by one remove: in the case above, uncle = walrus and everything falls into place neatly enough.

The meaning of dreams

Why bother with this kind of dream analysis at all? Because it is plain that meanings are sometimes disguised; because when thinking further about the dream, you may well recall some more of it; and because the elements of the dream which are *not* readily explained away may be of particular significance. Dream images or impressions which really are inexplicable may be the most likely to show ESP at work. Here is another specific example of the 'unusual response' principle at work.

Dream clairvoyance

A dream clairvoyance experiment is the simplest type of dream psi experiment to do, and results with such experiments have been promising.

To do this experiment, you will need a set of four diverse pictures, as in a standard picture-guessing test (see Chapter 5). You'll also need a thick, opaque envelope – a padded mailing envelope is perfect – large enough to contain any of those four pictures. And you'll need someone to act as randomizer to select one of the pictures as the target. Follow the procedure given. You should have your own judging set of pictures as before.

EXPERIMENT 2: DREAM CLAIRVOYANCE

You need a set of four pictures in separate numbered envelopes and duplicates, as explained on pp. 85–92 and a padded envelope. Arrange for a friend to act as randomizer.

1 The randomizer selects a target picture using the random-selection method (see p.85). He places the chosen picture (inside its envelope) in the padded envelope and staples it closed.

2 The randomizer arranges for the parcel containing the target to be sent to the subject and keeps the remaining three pictures. The subject does not meet the randomizer after he has chosen the picture; this way he cannot pick up stray clues.

3 On going to bed, the subject places the package on the beside table or under the pillows – he should make a conscious effort to dream about what's inside.

4 In the morning, the subject recalls as much as possible of the dreams, and makes a note of it.

5 Judge as for an ordinary picture test, using the judging set.

Scoring the results can be done exactly as for ordinary picture-guessing tests, using the number of direct hits scored or the more sensitive rank-sum analysis, as shown on pp. 97–98.

Before you start any dream ESP tests, you should practise by carrying out informal dream-recall sessions alone without any ESP testing, until you do have a reasonable rate of dream recall; recalling at least some dreams 50 per cent of the time. And, as with ganzfeld testing (Chapter 7), you can't expect statistically significant results from a handful of tests. About 30 would be a reasonable number, but you can choose whatever number you like. After all, this is for your interest; it's not a laboratory experiment.

As with ganzfeld picture tests, you may find common themes which recur. Place relatively little weight on very common dream images or themes; since they are in most dreams, and by definition can't contain much in the way of an ESP effect.

Dream telepathy

This is a relatively straightforward modification of the
dream clairvoyance experiment. The steps involved are
as follows.

EXPERIMENT 3: DREAM TELEPATHY

You need the usual materials for picture-guessing and
a sender. If possible, find a sender who goes to bed later
than you do; the sender has to look at the picture while
you are asleep. If not, get someone to look at the target
shortly before your bedtime.

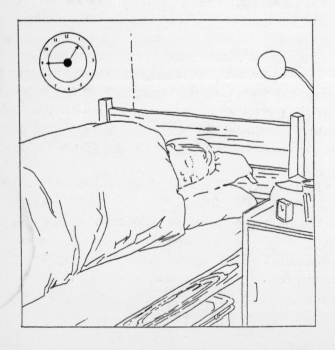

1 The sender selects the target as for experiment 1. Instead of sending it to the subject, the sender looks at the picture for 15 minutes at a pre-arranged time.

2 In the morning, the subject recalls his dreams.

3 The subject uses a judging set and makes his selection.

4 The subject contacts the sender to discover the true identity of the target.

5 Score your results as for experiment 1.

If you don't recall any dreams on the night of the experiment, try again using a new target (set of pictures?).

Final comments

If you do start dream-ESP testing, on nights when you
aren't doing a test, do try and keep your dream diary
going the next day – try to recall your dreams even if
you don't need them for any ESP testing. A well-kept
dream diary will ensure you don't get out of practice at
recalling your dreams, and also will show you, by looking back over it, which elements in your dreams are
common themes – the ones you can pay least attention
to in the judging. Also, the dream diary is of interest in
itself; it may be used to study possible dream precognition with everyday events, as we shall see later.

7

ESP Testing in the Twilight Zone

There is considerable evidence to show that relaxation, relief from distractions, R-mode activity, spontaneous and original mental activity, and what may loosely be called 'altered states of consciousness' are favourable for ESP. In this chapter we show how to do ESP picture-guessing experiments in a mild and pleasant 'altered state' using the ganzfeld procedure (*Ganzfeld* is a German word meaning 'uniform field' – the reasons for this label will become clear shortly). The procedure was devised by, and the most remarkable results with it have come from, Charles Honorton (now at Princeton but originally at the Maimonides Medical Center in Brooklyn) and there is now evidence from 12 independent laboratories around the world to show that his procedure is strongly favourable for ESP.

Honorton's ganzfeld procedure

A telepathy experiment is used, rather than a clairvoyance design, so three people are involved: a sender, a receiver and an experimenter. The procedure is as follows: in one (soundproofed) room, the receiver lies on a reclining chair and makes himself comfortable. The experimenter then sets up the ganzfeld: he puts headphones on the receiver, through which is relayed white noise – sound spread equally over all frequencies in the audible spectrum; over the receiver's eyes are placed halved ping-pong balls, packed around with cotton wool and kept in place with adhesive tape, through which gentle red light is diffused. At first things seem blotchy, but before long one is swimming in a sea of warm and homogeneous orange/red light. In this state, the receiver gives a verbal report on the images and impressions he has of the target picture; experienced receivers learn to pace this so that they disturb themselves as little as possible. Honorton has coined the word *mentation* to mean the receiver's mental activity in ganzfeld. The experimenter records what the subject says, by writing it down or taping it or both. This continues for 30 minutes. During this time, the sender is located in another room and is looking at the randomly selected target picture (as in a standard picture-guessing ESP test, see pp. 88–90), chosen from a set of four.

At the end of the test period, the results are judged and scored as in the standard picture-guessing experiment (see pp. 96–98).

Why ganzfeld?

If the old idea of ESP being a 'sixth sense' has any

validity, then it must operate as a weak one compared to our much stronger senses of seeing and hearing and so on: the signals are drowned out in the brain. If we could 'turn off' the strong sensory inputs, we may detect ESP signals more readily. This would explain why relaxation (no distracting body-movement and muscle-tension signals), and such factors as hypnosis and the dream state (see Chapter 6) are ESP-favourable.

How does ganzfeld work?

By playing a trick on the brain. It is not necessary to cut out strong sensory input to the brain altogether. If we simply keep the incoming signals *constant*, then after a while the brain simply gives up attending. Nothing new is happening, nothing changes; no information, so no monitoring. Under these conditions the attention of the brain tracks off on to internal factors, imagery and imagination.

So what is it like to be a guinea-pig with this technique? Certainly interesting and usually very relaxing. *Physical* changes may be fairly marked: the body may feel light, insubstantial, even floating or heavy; warm or cold or tingly. *Mental* effects can vary a lot. Some individuals report strong visual imagery, while others do not. Some people find they can hear strong alterations in the noise – they can hear wind, surf, rain, trains, people talking, music, crunching potato crisp bags – very varied impressions. But few people find the experience anything other than pleasant, and if the conditions for testing are right, it can be delightful.

Preparation
You'll need the following materials for conducting
ganzfeld ESP sessions.

1 A number of different sets of four pictures as used
   in standard ESP picture-guessing experiments, in
   duplicate sets.
2 Pencils, paper and a tape recorder if you have one –
   it may be easier to record results in this way rather
   than writing them down.
3 Two rooms, preferably not adjacent – e.g. front
   downstairs and back upstairs. Rooms in two different houses are even better. A comfortable couch or
   mattress for the receiver to lie on.
4 Sender, receiver and experimenter.
5 Equipment for visual and auditory ganzfeld.

Finally, before conducting an ESP test session with the
ganzfeld, it is strongly advisable to try a 'dummy session' – a ganzfeld session without any form of ESP test,
just trying out the procedure to see what it feels like,
what your reactions are, without any pressure or feeling
that any kind of test is involved in any way.

Visual ganzfeld
You'll need a pair of ping-pong balls, cotton wool and
adhesive tape. Cut the ping-pong balls in half, throwing
away the halves with the maker's name on them. Sand
the edges down until they're *perfectly* smooth. (People
with contact lenses should remove them at this point.)

Gently place a ping-pong ball half over the right eye and get the receiver to position it so that it's comfortable. Then pack around it with cotton wool until the field of vision in the right eye is completely obscured, and gently tape in place. Certain brands of tape are better as they come off very easily and comfortably. Repeat for the left eye.

After attaching the ping-pong balls, the experimenter should check with the receiver that they're comfortable and that there are no gaps round the edges of the field of vision, if the receiver looks straight ahead. At this stage the visual field will certainly look blotchy, which will change later.

The experimenter then positions the red light source (an anglepoise lamp is perfect) so that when the other lights in the room are extinguished (if running a session during the daytime, draw the curtains), the receiver sees a red light which is neither too bright, nor too dim. For a 60-watt red light source, somewhere between 12 and 24 inches (30 and 60 cm) above the face is the range within which most receivers select a value. The receiver should keep it in mind that the light will seem slightly dimmer after a few minutes of ganzfeld, so it shouldn't be *too* dim to start with. When this has been arranged to the receiver's satisfaction, put the main lights on again, and complete preparations.

Auditory ganzfeld

You may have problems creating white noise. It is possible that you know an electrical engineering or electronics firm which can make up the equipment for you. If you can, you'll want to relay this signal through headphones via an amplifier with tone and volume controls (no special amplifier facilities are needed). Otherwise, you can use a radio or tuner tuned between stations, but the noise isn't truly random, without structure, and is often not pleasant to listen to. Another possibility is to use a noisy blank tape played over an old, noisy amplifier – you should filter out the low (bass) frequencies as these make the sound slightly unpleasant to some people. With a powerful amplifier, the internal noise of the amplifier alone may be loud enough to provide an adequate source of white noise – just turn the amplifier function control to 'phono', don't put in any input and turn up the volume. After the receiver has put on the headphones, the experimenter should gradually adjust the volume to be loud enough but comfortable, and then make it slightly louder as the sound will appear to fade a little after the first few minutes. If none of these sources are available, it is best to have silence – use earplugs.

You need three people

For telepathy tests, you need a receiver, a sender and an experimenter. A ganzfeld session will often last a good hour or more, so make sure people have time to spare. The sender, in particular, may have to sit quietly for periods of up to an hour between finishing sending and being called in to reveal the target. It isn't feasible to sit doing nothing for that period of time as you'll get very bored. Try to stick to neutral activities: some senders read psychology books, which they find neutral and sometimes tedious; receivers never precognize anything from these books.

The experimenter can either be in the room with the receiver or just outside, depending on the receiver's performance. He must be within earshot to record what the receiver says.

EXPERIMENT 4: GANZFELD TELEPATHY PICTURE-GUESSING TEST

You will need all the equipment used in experiment 1 plus the apparatus described in Preparation.

1 The receiver is set up in ganzfeld in room 1 by the experimenter in the presence of the sender.

2 The sender and experimenter synchronize watches and record the time. The main room lights are extinguished (time 0).

3 The sender goes to room 2. The experimenter stays in room 1 or is just outside, but must be within earshot of the receiver, and not within earshot of the sender.

4 After 10 minutes (time 10), the sender randomly selects a target (see p. 86). He 'sends' the target for 10 minutes, finishing 20 minutes after the session commences (time 20). The sender then waits for

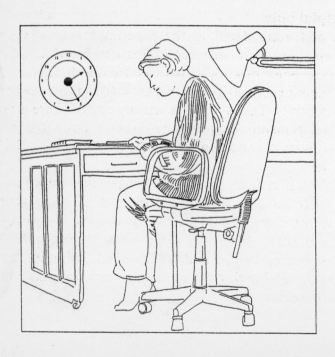

the experimenter to summon him to room 1 (maybe as long as an hour; see Preparation).

5 The experimenter records the receiver's mentation for 30 minutes, commencing time 0 (see Helpful hints).

6 Time 30. The experimenter signals the end of the session by turning on the main lights and slowly turning down the white noise. The receiver removes the headphones and ping-pong balls.

7 The receiver readjusts for as long as necessary and the experimenter starts judging (see Helpful hints).

8 The sender is then called in to reveal the target. Results are scored and recorded.

Helpful hints

To add extra detail to the experimental procedure given above, here are some suggestions based on a lot of experience in working with ganzfeld technique.

1 Don't be in any rush to report images if you are the receiver. Take your time settling down. There is no relationship between how many impressions receivers get and how successful they are in the ESP test.

2 You may find, if you 'see' images, that they naturally tend to appear, get more detailed in your mind's eye, and then finally fade away. When you talk about the images to the experimenter, wait for the image to form and fade – then talk about it. This way, talking shouldn't interfere much with the flow of imagery.

3 Don't censor anything – report all you can.

4 Receivers shouldn't make any effort to try and think about the sender – the whole point about ganzfeld is that the receiver should be passive.

5 Don't act as sender or receiver more than once a day, although the same experimenter could run more than one session a day. Nor should you act as sender for one session, and receiver for another in the same day, as material from the target in one session may be picked up by the receiver in another.

6 There is evidence which suggests that *auditory* imagery or unusual images are particularly likely to contain target-related material – pay attention to these aspects when judging.

7 Don't run a session if the receiver is ill or has been using any drugs or alcohol.

Scoring the results

You can't realistically expect significant results from too small a number of tests; and in a controlled laboratory study an experimenter has to specify exactly how many sessions he will include in an experiment in advance before checking and scoring the results. Most ganzfeld researchers would consider 30 sessions an adequate number for showing a significant result, but that's time-consuming. A series with as few as 10 or 20 tests should clearly give a better than chance result, although perhaps not a significant one.

Results can be checked exactly as for standard

picture-guessing (see pp. 96–98) using the direct-hit rate, or the sum of ranks measure.

Modified tests

Two-person telepathy experiment: This experiment can be used if it isn't convenient or practical to have three people involved. The sender can set the receiver up in ganzfeld and then leave him on his own, with no experimenter. The receiver can tape-record his spoken impressions and after the session can use them in judging; to time the session an alarm clock is necessary (a nasty surprise!). After the judging, the receiver can fetch the sender to discover the target and score the results.

This is a viable procedure, although it has been noticed that receivers left on their own tend to be rather more nervous than receivers with an experimenter. So this two-person procedure may be less likely to give good results than the three-person telepathy procedure.

Three-person clairvoyance experiment: It is possible to run such an experiment by a straightforward change in the telepathy procedure. There is no sender, but a randomizer (who cannot be the experimenter or receiver in the session!) who chooses the target picture in advance, but does *not* open the envelope with the target picture in it. Instead, the envelope containing the target picture should be sealed up in a padded envelope labelled 'Target', and left in a safe place for the experimenter and subject to locate after judging.

Other features of free-response tests

Two other features of free-response tests worth mentioning are as follows:

1 One sometimes gets very accurate descriptions by receivers of pictures. In these cases the probability of the hit is obviously better than 1 in 4 (25 per cent chance) judging would suggest. So, a series of sessions which doesn't give significant results *overall* may nonetheless contain one or more very strong, detailed *individual* hits.

2 Spontaneous ESP between the individuals involved in test sessions appears to become more common, both in the sessions and outside. In test sessions themselves, spontaneous ESP between sender and receiver may be common: the sender's thoughts may wander from the target picture and this is picked up by the receiver. If you keep the records from sessions (copies of receiver's spoken report, and so on) make a note of such occurrences on a sheet of paper and keep this record of spontaneous ESP with the formal data on the experiment.

8

Precognition Testing

Precognition, knowledge of future events acquired by ESP, is certainly the most astonishing and intriguing aspect of psi. Oddly enough, there has not been so much laboratory research into precognition as into PK, telepathy or clairvoyance, but there is some impressive evidence to be found. The strongest results come from a dream precognition experiment series conducted at Maimonides Medical Center with a single subject, the English psychic Malcolm Bessent. Although complex, the design of the experiment centred on Bessent's ability to dream about events of the next day, which would be determined from the nature of a randomly selected target picture. On one occasion the target picture chosen (after Bessent's dreams) showed a mental hospital corridor; Bessent was treated as a mental patient the next morning by the experimenters. His dreams, with references to doctors, escaping patients, and so on, clearly incorporated the target material. The formal, statistical measurement in this experiment was made by sending to independent judges Bessent's dreams, plus the target and seven 'control' (non-target) pictures, for each night. Thus, Bessent had a 1 in 8 chance of being correct by guesswork for each night of the series (of 16 tests). Instead of the two hits expected (16 × 1/8), Bessent obtained 10. The odds against this remarkable performance being due to chance are over 100,000 to 1.

There is also much evidence for precognition from spontaneous psi. Reported precognitions of famous disasters like the Aberfan mining disaster, the Flixborough chemical plant explosion and aircraft crashes are not uncommon. Obviously, as with any spontaneous case evidence, the possibility of coincidence cannot entirely be ruled out, but sometimes the details of reported precognitions are sufficiently accurate for coincidence to be an unconvincing explanation.

Although most of this chapter is concerned with precognition experiments, J. W. Dunne's book *An Experiment with Time* suggests a method for stimulating spontaneous precognition in dreams which is worth discussing.

Precognition in dreams

Published in 1927, *An Experiment with Time* suggests two key strategies for stimulating spontaneous dream precognition. First, increase dream recall; Dunne's suggestions are very similar to ours: wake up promptly and write down or record the dream material you can

remember. Dunne urges the dreamer to fix his attention on what he has recalled and try to recall extra,
possibly corroborative detail. Second, analyse the
dream properly, and pay attention to details.

Dunne's belief was that dreams incorporate material
from the past and the future, possibly in almost equal
proportions and that if examined carefully this be-
comes apparent. Dunne suggested that there are certain
blocks involved, reasons why we don't see precognitive
elements. The major ones are:

1 Inadequate attention to the details of dreams.
2 Too-ready dismissal of 'trivial' correspondence between a dream and future events.
3 A 'resistance' to the idea of precognition; a non-in-
   tentional failure to notice correspondence.

Dunne's thesis was that, if one kept a dream diary for
some weeks, and analysed it exhaustively – comparing
the events of each day with the dreams *before and after*
it – one would find as many links between dreams and
events following them as one would between dreams
and events preceding them. Dunne (probably correctly) felt that many people could not accept this radi-
cal view and suggested a neat psychological trick:
pretend that a dream which precedes a day, where
you're looking for possible precognitions in the dream
of the events of the day, actually *followed* it. If you do
this, resistance to the idea of dream precognition is by-
passed, and correspondences become clearer.

Dunne's own results came from a small circle of friends and, mostly, from his own dreams. He certainly seems to have precognized many events, from the fairly trivial, commonplace (but, Dunne stresses, *don't* ignore these; ignoring them is part of a resistance to the idea of precognition) to major events. One example was the eruption of a volcano in Martinique in 1902, of which he dreamed vividly beforehand, and likewise the progress of an African exploring party when he was stationed in Italy.

His results are often not given in enough detail: for example, when Dunne claims to have dreamed in advance of newspaper headlines, he does not give exact dates. And his theory about the nature of time ('Serial Time') is ridiculous: even in 1927 it was decidedly half-baked. But his material isn't sensationalized; and he does discuss the importance of detail and *unusual* events during dreams (he suggests that such events are most likely to provide evidence of precognition, a view amply supported since).

In 1950, a book appeared which suggested that studious application of Dunne's technique (stimulate dream recall, analyse carefully, regularly go back over old dreams checking for possible precognitions) was useful, John Godley, now Lord Kilbracken, in his *Tell me the Next One* (Gollancz, 1950), gives an account of how he regularly dreamed of horse-race winners and of how he notified his friends so that precise dates, witnessing, etc., are available. There are similarities with Dunne; thus Kilbracken, like Dunne, often dreamed of newspaper headlines rather than the events themselves. Kilbracken's best coup was notifying a national newspaper in one case of a 'double'! Of his 10 'dream winners', eight won; and one of the others should not have been counted, for he had already backed it, and this was almost certainly a wish-fulfilment dream. In any case, an 80 per cent hit rate would certainly be enough to keep a newspaper tipster or punter very happy!

Precognition with cards

In this simple precognition experiment the aim is to try and shuffle a pack of cards so that the order is similar to that of a pack of cards which will be shuffled *later*. Again you may improve your results by using the relaxation techniques beforehand.

EXPERIMENT 5: PRECOGNITION WITH CARDS

You need two packs of playing cards with the jokers removed and a friend to act as randomizer. It is better to use packs with different backs. Randomizer and guesser should be in different rooms and have no contact before scoring the results.

1 Arrange a time sequence with the randomizer. The subject should shuffle the guess pack at a fixed time (time 0) and the randomizer, the target pack, after a fixed interval (15 minutes is suitable to start with: time 15). Record the chosen time interval.

2 Time 0. The subject sits down with the guess pack
   and idly shuffles them. It is better not to concentrate or make much effort; continue until you 'feel'
   you have a 'good' order. Place the pack somewhere
   where it will be undisturbed.

3 Time 15. The randomizer shuffles the target pack
   in a similar fashion, without looking at the guess
   pack.

4 The randomizer relays the target pack to the
   subject.

5 Score the results. Turn over the first card in the
   guess pack and record its identity: 2H for 2 of
   hearts, AS for the ace of spades, and so on. Do the
   same for the target pack and record the card's identity in a second column so that there are two rows
   of figures: guesses and targets. Continue until all 52
   cards in each pack have been recorded. Cross check
   by making sure that you have each of the 52 different cards in each column.

The results can be scored differently depending on the
aim of the experiment. If your experiment was simply
for prediction of red or black, then you should score the
results as explained on p. 62 for a 1 in 2 test; if your
experiment was for prediction of suit rather than colour, then turn to p. 68 for the 1 in 4 score key.

Variations on the procedure
The following modification to this experiment will
make it more controlled, but takes a lot of extra time.

The subject follows exactly the same procedure as above, shuffling the pack. But the randomizer does *not* shuffle the second pack. Rather, he puts the cards in a random order, using Table V of random numbers as follows (if black-red, colour-guessing design is being used):

> 1, 3, 5, 7, 9 = any red card
> 2, 4, 6, 8, 0 = any black card

Go on until you have ordered all 52 cards. Of course, you will run out of one colour first so you will be left with cards all of the other colour – simply complete the sequence with these few remaining cards. Obviously, the task will be easier if you separate the 52 cards into two stacks – red and black – in advance. Do not arrange them in any kind of numerical sequence before you begin the random-choosing procedure. This true-random pack is then given to the subject. For a suit-guessing test, use the random numbers to order the targets thus:

> 1,5 = any heart
> 2,6 = any club
> 3,7 = any diamond
> 4,8 = any spade
> 9,0 = ignore

Again, you will find that you run out of certain suits – all 13 cards of the suit will be in the target pack. If the next digit from the random number table shows a target suit which is exhausted, ignore it and continue reading off from the table.

The scoring is done exactly the same as for the two-shuffle test.

Precognition without cards

A third type of test of this kind is also a little more time-consuming but uses a different guessing strategy. Allow more time between guessing and randomizing, since a subject may take more than 15 minutes to guess. You will not, as subject, need a pack of cards here. Simply sit and relax at the arranged time and try to guess one at a time the order of cards in the pack, writing down your guesses on a sheet of paper.

The randomizer may prepare the targets by shuffling or from the random-number tables. Again, you can try colour guessing or suit guessing, and score the results as before (p. 68 for colour guessing, p. 62 for suit guessing).

In all cases, keep a careful record of the experiments you do, when they were done and what time interval separated guessing from the production of the targets.

Precognition with pictures

You will need duplicate sets of four different pictures, and other standard material for picture-guessing tests (see Chapter 5). Again, two people are involved: a subject and a randomizer. A time schedule will be needed in advance of the session. If you are acting as subject, it is worthwhile trying the following techniques.

Relax somewhere comfortable where you won't be disturbed for a while, close your eyes, and let your mind wander. Try to see in your mind's eye a blank wall, and if you can a clock, showing the time when you will see the target as arranged with the randomizer. What images appear on that wall? What forms appear on the blank canvas?

EXPERIMENT 6: PRECOGNITION WITH PICTURES

1 The subject and randomizer arrange the time sequence. The following is a good scheme: the subject tries to receive the target for 15 minutes (time 0 to time 15) and the randomizer selects a target from a pre-selected set at a fixed interval after this, say 45 minutes later (time 60). The subject arranges to meet the randomizer at time 65.

2 The randomizer selects the picture *set* to be used (see p. 90 for random-selection procedure). He does not select the target yet.

3 The randomizer writes the identity of the set on a slip of paper, seals it in an opaque envelope and hands it to the subject. The randomizer does not now see the subject until after the experiment.

4 Time 0. The subject spends 15 minutes meditating with the sealed envelope to gain an impression of the target. He writes or tapes notes.

5 Time 15. The subject opens the envelope to find out

which set was chosen and judges his notes using a duplicate picture set. The subject waits for the pre-arranged time (time 65) to discover the target identity.

6 Time 60. The randomizer selects the target following standard procedure (p. 85).

7 The randomizer displays the selected target so that the subject sees only this on entering the room at time 65 (should be a private room where the target won't be disturbed).

8 The results are scored.

The results of picture-guessing precognition experiments can be scored in exactly the same way as with ordinary picture tests, using the direct-hit and sum-of-ranks methods (pp. 96–97). Because there has been relatively little work with precognitive picture guessing of this kind, the expected success rate is not certain. A series of tests of some 20 sessions should, however, show a significant or nearly significant result with a moderately good subject.

Precognition in ganzfeld

The basic precognitive picture-guessing test can be adapted for use as a ganzfeld precognition experiment or a dream precognition experiment. As a ganzfeld precognition experiment, simply add the ganzfeld condition to the subject's role as given above. Here, you will need a third person – the experimenter – to whom the randomizer should supply the envelope containing the identity of the picture set to be used in the session. And the experimenter can keep a record of the subject's impressions and ideas, as spoken aloud. With a ganz-feld precognition experiment, there will *not* be a sender as in the standard ganzfeld telepathy experiment; there is a randomizer instead. The length of the session should be increased since experiments indicate that, for success, the duration of ganzfeld should be around 30 minutes. The results can be scored exactly as for a standard four-choice picture-guessing test.

Dreaming precognition

The procedure is as follows. The subject should record his dreams for the test night in the morning as usual. The randomizer should select a picture set for use in judging in the morning (i.e. after the subject's dreams) and pass on the identity of the target set to the subject. The subject should then use that set in judging. Later, the randomizer should randomly select the target *picture* (i.e. one of the four pictures in the picture set being used in the session) and display this in the fixed loca-tion at the arranged time, as in the standard precogni-tive picture-guessing procedure (experiment 6).

In this dream precognition design has a slight differ-ence from the others we have already looked at. Here, the set of pictures is chosen after the subject has 'guessed', whereas in the other experiments the set of pictures is chosen in advance. The target picture, of course, is always chosen after the subject's guesses have been made. It has been suggested that precognition may work better when the picture set has not been made up when the guesses are made (as is the case with the dream precognition experiment), since it is not possible for the subject's ESP to get sidetracked on to one of the 'wrong' pictures in the picture set (i.e. one of the three non-targets), but this has not convincingly been demonstrated as yet.

The results of the dream precognition experiment can be scored exactly as for standard, four-choice picture guessing (pp. 96–97).

So what is precognition?

It may have occurred to some of you that success can come about in the above experiments from a psi effect other than precognition. For example, take the simple two-shuffled pack precognition test right at the start of this chapter. Is it the case that the subject is using precognition to shuffle the first pack into the 'right' order? Or could the subject use PK on the randomizer's pack to make it conform with the first pack? Or could the randomizer use clairvoyance to read off the order of cards in the first pack, and to shuffle his to match it?

Even convincing laboratory evidence of precognition, which shows that some psi effect must be present (like the experiments with Malcolm Bessent), cannot prove that precognition rather than another psi effect was involved. Perhaps Bessent used PK to influence which targets were selected. Where precognition cannot be denied (if we take such evidence seriously, as surely we must) is in the case of spontaneous, real-life precognition. When precognitions of major disasters occur, then they must indeed be precognitions: the only other explanation (apart from coincidence) is PK, and if PK can generate explosions, air crashes, mining disasters, earthquakes and (maybe) wars, no one is safe!

Influencing the future

But if precognition does exist, what implications are there for our view of time and free will? These are much too extensive to be discussed fully here, but one thing which can be stated is that if precognition does exist, the future may not be immune to alteration at will. Precognition is clearly *not* perfectly accurate; even in cases of spontaneous precognition which are dramatic, some details are often wrong. When J. W. Dunne had a precognition of a newspaper headline concerning a volcanic eruption, the headline proclaimed 40,000 dead: Dunne dreamed of the number 4000. Also, Dunne did not recognize the precise location of the disaster. There are always mistakes and omissions and it may be that precognition foretells the most likely outcome in the future of unknown events occurring now. Thus the future isn't black and white certainties, but shades of grey likelihoods which are certainly not alterable.

The experiments suggested in this book, to date, almost all concern tests to see if ESP is present overall in the results. We have been comparing the scoring rate in experiments against chance to see if they are clearly different, thus suggesting psi at work. However, in the next chapter the experiments concern a different comparison: comparing the results of different ESP tests – tests completed under different conditions, by different subjects, and so on. We want to know if ESP scores vary regularly, under different conditions. Which kinds of people (if any) have clearly better psi scores than other people? Does psi ability fluctuate with mood? This is the psychology of psi.

9

The Psychology of Psi

In the first section, we suggest experiments which compare ESP test scores from the *same person* under *different conditions*. Such results tell us a lot about the psychology of the individual's psi. The second section concerns experiments in which results from ESP tests are completed by *different people* under *the same conditions*. With such experiments, we are asking a more general question about psi: what aspects of the psychology of psi are true for most people? The first type of experiment, however, is obviously more convenient and if results obtained by several individuals, working independently are similar then we wouldn't think them necessarily idiosyncratic.

You will be using several of the procedures of tests described in earlier chapters. Although you can use the score keys given, if you conduct a suitable number of tests, you may find it helpful to derive your own score keys. Go back to Chapter 2 for the method. We suggest that you do not try these experiments until you have practised with the earlier ones.

SOLO EXPERIMENTS

Mood and psi
The question being asked in this test is whether ESP scoring is significantly different when an individual is in a good, as versus a bad, mood? Any type of ESP test in this book can be used, but our example concerns the use of simple, colour guessing with playing cards (Game 1 on pp. 60–63), since this is a quick experiment to do.

EXPERIMENT 7: MOOD AND PSI

1 Decide on the number of test sessions. Ten is adequate.
2 Record your mood: good or bad. Don't change it afterwards!
3 Follow procedure for Game 1 (p. 60). Repeat this a further 4 times. (You have made 50 guesses in all.)
4 Repeat Steps 2 and 3 until you have completed the number of sessions decided on (9 times in this case).

Your score card: 1 in 2 colour guessing

Good mood							
Bad mood							

Total number of guesses:

For each session of tests, you will have a total score between 0 and 50, with a chance average of 25, as this is a 1 in 2 test ★ • . How does mood affect your scores?

Your score card might look like this:

Good mood	22	31	30	24	33	30	6 sessions, 170 hits
Bad mood		29	17	22	23		4 sessions, 91 hits

Total number of guesses: 500

In this case, our subject has been in a good mood slightly more often than in a bad mood; this is all right, a subject does not have to be in each mood exactly half the time.

First, compare each of the two scores (GM and BM) with the chance average score. For the GM scores, there are six sessions: a chance average is 6 × 25 (**the chance average per test**), which is **150. The** *actual* **score was 170;**

★ If you are unsure of the chance scores for tests, consult the tables in Appendix 1 under the columns headed 'Chance'. Be careful to use the appropriate table.

record this as +20. The BM score was 92; by chance you would expect 4 × 25, or 100: score –9. You must record your score in this way, rather than simply subtracting one score from the other, as you may be doing unequal numbers of tests in each mood.

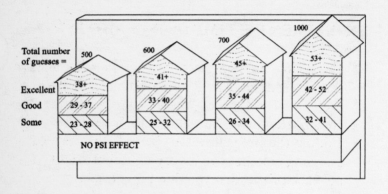

Total number of guesses = 500

GM score = +20

BM score = –9

Difference = (+20) - (-9) = 29

The important thing with this test is to keep a full record of tests, rating moods as good or bad in advance; you should complete at least a few tests in each mood.

Time of day and psi

There is remarkably little research on time of day of testing and psi ability but what few reports exist suggest it may be a strong effect to look at. Again, any type of ESP test can be used; in this example we use a 1 in 4 suit-guessing game.

EXPERIMENT 8: TIME OF DAY AND PSI

1 Decide on the number of test sessions. Do half in the morning and half in the evening. Try five of each.
2 Record the time at the start of each session.
3 Follow the procedure for Game 1, but instead of guessing colours, you are trying to guess suits. Label each pile so that you don't lose track.
4 Repeat Step 3 until you have completed the number of sessions decided on.

Your score card: 1 in 4 suit guessing

Morning						
Evening						

Total number of guesses:

You might end up with results like this:

Morning	13	10	14	15	16	5 sessions, 68 hits
Evening	11	11	10	14	12	5 sessions, 58 hits

Total number of guesses = 500

Since the chance score for each is the same – there are the same number of tests at each time of day – we simply compare the scores directly:

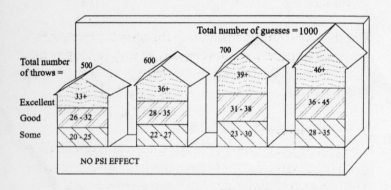

Difference: 10 and this result is not significant

We conclude, therefore, that time of day does not affect psi ability. Perhaps you can score better – the difference found might be greater if the tests are done as early in the morning and as late in the evening as possible.

More controlled tests
Experiments 7 and 8 can be made more controlled by making the following changes in the design:

1 Have a randomizer prepare the targets for each session, keeping a record of the order as dictated by the random number tables.
2 Have the targets sealed in opaque envelopes.
3 Have the guesser write down his guesses, guessing the order of a complete target pack – 10 cards – at a time.

Whether you toughen up the conditions using these revisions depends on how much time you've got and whether you're bothered about the test being well controlled or not.

Does PK decline?
It has often been reported that when a single PK dice-throwing session is conducted, the PK scoring tends to start very well and then fall away – the *decline effect*. This simple experiment, based on Game 7 (p. 77), will enable you to test for yourself.

EXPERIMENT 9: DOES PK DECLINE?

1 in 6 Sevens Test

1 Decide on the number of sessions. This time, try six.

2 Follow the procedure given for Game 7 on p. 77. Do this 10 times, putting your scores in one column. Repeat five times, each time starting a new column. At the end you should have six columns with 10 entries in each.

3 Repeat Step 2 five times. The total number of throws will be 360.

4 Discard the middle 20 throws in each session.

5 You will be left with 120 'start' and 120 'end' trials.

Your score card: 1 in 6 dice throwing

Total throws (excluding 'middle' trials) <u>240</u>

   'Start' hits _____

   'End' hits _____

   Difference_____

If a decline effect is strong then the scoring on the first trials should be higher than on the end trials; perhaps this is a cut and dried version of 'beginner's luck'. The total number of trials being considered is 240, and since there is the same number of start and end trials, we can just compare their scores directly. What if the start trials gave 29 hits and the end trials 15?

Difference = 29 — 15
= 14

From the score key we see that the answer shows some evidence of a significant difference.

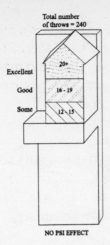

It has often been thought that declines may be due to boredom, fatigue, and similar factors. If this is true, the best test conditions under which to show declines would be ones in which the subject was fairly tired and fatigued to start with, so that initial enthusiasm waned fairly fast.

Although, in the example above, six sessions is suggested, 10 might be a better number to use in order to show a decline clearly. One point we should clarify is that it is *not* wrong to throw away the results of the middle 20 trials from each session; *providing one plans to do this in advance of the experiment.* They are discarded in the PK test to make a sharper comparison between start and end trials.

Relaxation and psi
The first experiment studies ESP performance under conditions of relaxation versus non-relaxation. The second explores the effects of regular use of relaxation techniques in the long term: possibly a learning effect.

Relaxation versus non-relaxation
In this experiment, you are trying to perform a series of tests; half of them in each condition, but randomly ordered. You will aim to do one test each day, the whole experiment lasting 10 days.

EXPERIMENT 10: RELAXATION AND PSI

You can conduct this experiment by yourself, but you must make sure that you use the same test throughout. We suggest a 1 in 4 suit-guessing test.
1 Decide on the number of tests. You need to make at least 100 guesses in each test and five tests for each of the relaxed and non-relaxed conditions. The total guesses will be 1000.
2 Use either shuffled packs or true-random packs (see p. 131).
3 Perform one test a day, preferably at the same time. Try not to leave long intervals between tests; although it is all right to miss the odd day. Which test you do on which day should be determined using random numbers (1, 3, 5, 7, 9 = relaxation; 2, 4, 6, 8, 0 = non-relaxation). For non-relaxation tests, conduct them in the usual way; for relaxation tests,

go through the progressive relaxation procedure described on p. 47 and then do the tests soon after while you are still relaxed. The random order is used to discount the possibility of the decline effect coming into play (see p. 145 for an explanation).

4 Keep a careful record of your results and conditions.

Your score card: 1 in 4 suit guessing

| Relaxation | | | | | | ——sessions,——hits |
| No relaxation | | | | | | ——sessions,——hits |

Difference =

Total guesses =

Use a suitable number of tests so that you can score the results from Table II (refresh your memory from pp. 40–42.

Does relaxation improve ESP in the long run?

An experiment to examine this question is strictly for the enthusiast since by its very nature it must be time-consuming – a series of tests extending over several months (one a week) interspersed with regular relaxation exercises. Does relaxation training improve your psi ability.

EXPERIMENT 11: LONG-TERM RELAXATION

1 Decide which test you are going to use. We suggest
   suit guessing again.
2 Arrange a schedule: 12 weeks with one 200-test session each week, preferably on the same day and at
   the same time, under similar conditions. In this
   case there is no random ordering.
3 Do the relaxation exercises regularly and consis-
   tently throughout the experiment, except before
   the first one of the 12 tests. This will then serve as
   a baseline measure for the following 11. When following the relaxation routine for the latter, don't do
   the tests immediately after: you are checking for
   long-term effects, not immediate ones.

Your score card: 1 in 4 suit guessing

Session	1	2	3	4	5	6	Total
Score							
Session	7	8	9	10	11	12	Total
Score							

Score the results as for Experiment 10.

GROUP EXPERIMENTS
The experiments in this section all require a reasonable

number of participants; we suggest numbers for the different experiments. The question being asked is: what kinds of people have the highest psi ability? The experiments we suggest have been replicated many times and are among the most robust effects experimenters have yet found in parapsychology.

On occasions, you may be able to use the score keys, or the tables in Appendix 1. You will probably find, though, that the number of tests you carry out are too large, or fall between the round figures given. In these instances you must use the Z test in Appendix 2. To make life easier, we take you through various examples and show you what value to use in the equation. You will need a calculator that has a square-root function, or failing that, square-root tables.

Separating the sheep from the goats

Perhaps the most intuitively plausible, indeed obvious, finding about the psychology of psi ability is this: people who accept, or believe in the existence of psi (sheep) score better in ESP experiments than people who don't believe in psi, or even reject the possibility of its existing (goats). So, for this experiment, one needs to be able to find *both* kinds of person – both believers and disbelievers. The really violent sceptic – the person who flatly asserts that ESP is impossible – is nearly extinct now, and there is little point in looking for such people. But you probably do know some people who are confident that ESP does exist, and others who are very uncertain and think it probably doesn't.

The sheep-goat difference in psi testing is typically not very large. For this reason, if one wants to show a significant result, then you will need to test a reasonably-sized sample of people: this is an experiment for the enthusiast. It is *not* necessary to have exactly the same numbers of sheep and goats; but the *total* number of people you test should be at least 30.

EXPERIMENT 12: SHEEP AND GOATS

You need two packs of cards, a pen and some notepaper. Find somewhere comfortable for your 30 subjects to sit! (One at a time, of course.) You also need a randomizer to make up sets of 50 cards, randomly ordered, for each test.

1 The randomizer makes up the 50-card set. Keep this out of the subject's sight. If possible, sit across a table with a small screen.

2 Record the subject's name. Ask them if they believe in ESP. Some people will be uncertain; what do they believe on the whole?

3 Explain that you have a pack of 50 cards, in a red-black random sequence and that they must try to guess the colour order. Tell them that you will not be looking at the cards so better than chance results will be due to clairvoyance.

4 When the subject makes his first guess, write down in the column headed 'guesses'. Turn the first card face up. Record the target next to the guess. Tell the

subject whether they are right or wrong. Feedback like this keeps the subject interested.

5 Continue until all 50 cards have been guessed. Add up the total with the subject.

Your score card: 1 in 2 colour guessing

Sheep										
Goat										

Sheep							—— sessions,
							—— hits
Goat							—— sessions,
							—— hits

Total number of guesses:

With 30 subjects, and 50 guesses per subject, there would be a total of 1500 guesses in the experiment. This value exceeds the limits of Table I and any of the score keys derived from it, so we have to resort to the Z test. The following example will show you how it's done:

Sheep	27	29	18	30	32	30	27	22	20	25
Sheep	27	25	28	26	21	28	26	36	20	22

20 sessions, 519 hits

Goats	20	28	22	21	15	29	17	30	22	24

10 sessions 228 hits

P, test probability - $\frac{1}{2}$ (1 in 2)

Chance average for each test	$=$	number of guesses in each	$\times \frac{1}{2}$
	$=$	$50 \times \frac{1}{2}$	
	$=$	25	

| Chance average total for each type | $=$ | number of sessions | $\times$ | chance average for each session |

Sheep chance average total $= 20 \times 25 = 500$

Goats chance average total $= 10 \times 25 = 250$

Actual scores:

Sheep $= 519$ (19 more than chance)

Goats $= 228$ (22 less than chance)

Difference $= 19 - (-22) = 41$

Is this difference significant?
From the Z equation on p. 192 we get:

$$Z = \frac{41}{\sqrt{[1500 \times \frac{1}{2} \times (1 - \frac{1}{2}]}}$$

$$= 2.21$$

From the score key we can see that this value indicates *some* evidence of sheep-goat effect.

Effect on psi ability	Z value
Some	Greater than 1.95
Good	Greater than 2.57
Excellent	Greater than 3.29

If you were using a 1 in 4 suit-guessing test, P would be $\frac{1}{4}$ and $P - 1$, $\frac{3}{4}$. In this case:

$$Z = \frac{41}{\sqrt{(1500 \times \frac{1}{4} \times \frac{3}{4})}}$$

$$= 2.44$$

which would again indicate *some* evidence.

If you come across individuals who score significantly (although by chance you should expect one or two people from such a large sample to score extreme results), it may be worthwhile doing some more tests on them to see whether they are truly high scorers.

Other useful points of procedure are:

1   Treat all the subjects and test them in the same way.

For example, you might decide to alter the experimental design suggested above by having a break after 25 guesses, even though making 50 guesses doesn't take very long. If you do that, make sure you give all the subjects a break, unless any of them are vehement that they really *don't* want one. Don't, for example, change the testing conditions half-way through testing.

2 It's a good idea to run through the test with a friend, acting as a guinea-pig trial subject, to make sure everything goes smoothly and the experiment runs as it should.

3 Any psi test, in principle, can be used to look at the sheep-goat effect. The example given here is of a test which is fairly quick in that it should only take a few minutes to test each person, which is desirable if you are going to test 30 or so people. It would not be a good idea, for example, to use a dream ESP test since this is time-consuming.

4 Try and fix the number of guessers to be tested in advance of the experiment, but if it really isn't possible to test as many as you would have liked, then stop when convenient. In a controlled laboratory study, the number must be fixed and stuck with: but perhaps the last one or two people are hard to get hold of and you aren't doing a laboratory study. But, if it's possible, stick with the original intended number.

Extroverts and introverts and psi

Not only do sheep and goats differ in psi ability, but so
do extroverts and introverts. Usually, extroverts score
higher in ESP tests than introverts. There is a wealth
of evidence for this – 22 confirming studies from all
over the world – but why this should be so isn't certain.
It may be due to differences in brain activity in extroverts and introverts, or social factors (comfort in testing, etc.). But it is a real difference – and here is a
suggested experiment to look at the extrovert-introvert
difference.

EXPERIMENT 13: EXTROVERTS AND INTROVERTS

You will need all the materials as for Experiment 10.

1 Decide which sort of test you are going to conduct:
  colour guessing is fine. Be consistent throughout.
2 The randomizer makes up the packs as before.
3 Record the subject's name. Ask him to give answers
  to the first 30 questions in Part 2 of the Questionnaire (pp. 20–24). You should have already filled
  this in yourself. Do not score yet.
4 Conduct the test as for Experiment 10.
5 Record your results.
6 Check the extroversion scores.

Your score card:

Player no.	1	2	3	4	5	6	7	8	9	10	11	12	13
Score													
Questionnaire score													
Introvert/ Extrovert I or E													

14	15	16	17	18	19	20	21	22	23	24	25	26	27	28	29	30

No. of introverts:

No. of extroverts:

Introvert scores:

Extrovert scores:

Questionnaire scores

For the questions, there is a possible range of scores from zero (extreme introversion) to 60 (extreme extroversion), although very few people will score right at the extremes. To find the average score, simply add all 30 together and find the total; divide that total by 30. As an example:

Scores, 47, 13, 26, 32, 26, 32, 44, 28, 38, 39, 18, 22, 19, 27, 30, 28, 29, 30, 20, 21, 28, 50, 33, 37, 24, 26, 30, 39, 38, 22. Total: 896 Average: 896/30 = 29.87.

In this case, all subjects with scores of 30 or above would be classed as extroverts, and all those with scores of 29 or below would be classed as introverts. This gives us 14 extroverts and 16 introverts. We need to work out an average, because there is no known general-population average for the scale used in this book. It is a shorter version of a long personality questionnaire for which such averages are known. Group your scores like this:

Extroverts (14) ESP scores: 27, 38, 22, 19, 19, 28, 25, 27, 23, 21, 30, 30, 16, 28. Total score for group: 353 hits.

Introverts (16) ESP scores: 22, 29, 33, 17, 19, 22, 25, 20, 22, 18, 30, 32, 19, 20, 24. Total score for group: 372 hits.

In this case, with 50 guesses per subject in a 1 in 2 test, the chance average per subject is 25. The extroverts would therefore have scored 25 × 14 = 350 by chance. Their actual score is 353, just 3 above this; +3. For the introverts, a chance average group total would be 25 ö 16 = 400. Their actual score is 372, 28 less than this: -28. The difference between the two groups is thus 31.

Using the Z equation (p. 192), we get a Z value of 1.60.

Individual scores

The Z statistic tells us that there is a difference in scoring rates of two groups. But this difference may not be evenly distributed. It may be that you have two groups that appear to be different, but the difference is due to one or two extremely high-scoring individuals. If you feel that you are not getting a realistic assessment of the group's performance, you should try the *t* test explained in *Psychological Statistics* by Q. McNemar (John Wiley, 1962). On the other hand, you may turn your attention to carrying out more detailed tests on your Psi Stars!

10

The Psi Experiment

You are invited to participate in a major large-scale study of ESP. In our earlier book *Explaining the Unexplained* (Prion 1995) we included a small ESP test which elicited a great response. Here we include a more extensive and imaginative four-part test which, we hope, will give a more reliable measure of an individual's psi power.

Apart from some basic details, which you must supply, you are asked to complete four sub-tests and send in your completed questionnaire. You may do them in any order; if you don't wish to send in all of them, that is all right. However, the more complete results we get, the better a picture of ESP operating in this experiment we can obtain. You may also remain anonymous if you wish.

You can work through the sub-tests in any order you wish, but please record the date and time you did each one. We suggest that you either photocopy the test pages, or copy them out on to pieces of paper, if you want to keep the book intact, or detach the pages. Make sure that every sheet is carefully labelled.

The address you should mail your answers to is:

Dr C.L. Sargent, The Psychological Laboratory, University of Cambridge, Cambridge CB2 3EB (United Kingdom).

Please do *not* mail them to Professor Eysenck or the publishers of this book.

If your score is interesting, you will be contacted and asked if you would participate in further research into ESP, unless you indicate otherwise on your answer sheets.

Your name...

Address..

....

Sex (M or F)...

Your scores on the Psi questionnaire:

Part 1   General Belief (score between 0 and 12):
           Acceptance and Interest (score between 0 and 10):
           Personal Experience (score between 0 and 20):
           Survival and Religion (score between 0 and 24):

Part 2   Extroversion (score between 0 and 60):
           Anxiety (score between 0 and 60):

Part 3   Imagery and Imagination (score between 0 and 40):

Test 1

Imagine that the circle shown below is a radar screen. It is divided into 24 sections, and there is a 50% chance for each section in the radar screen that there is a 'blip' lurking in it, but you cannot actually *see* the screen. For this screen before you, a computer has generated a 'target screen' with the blips shown on it. What you have to do is to try and use ESP to guess which sections of the screen contain a blip in the computer-produced target. Put a cross in those sections which you think have a blip shown in them in that target screen.

Please note that you cannot do well in this test simply by filling in all the sections, since approximately half do *not* have a blip in them. After you've done the test – and don't take long over it – answer the questions below.

Questions

Tick one answer only for each question.

1   How relaxed did you feel when you did this test?
    Very relaxed
    Quite relaxed
    Neither relaxed nor tense

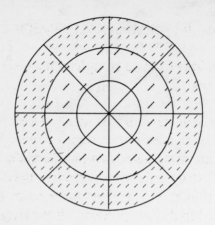

Quite tense
Very tense

2 What was your general mood like when you did this
   test?
   Very good
   Quite good
   Neutral
   Quite bad
   Very bad

3 How confident are you that you have used ESP in
   this test?
   Confident I've used ESP
   Feel it's likely I used ESP
   Uncertain
   Don't feel I used ESP
   Certain I didn't use ESP

On what date did you complete this test? ....

What time of day did you complete this test? ......am/pm

Test 2

Here is a list of 64 pairs of first names. In each pair, both names are either men's or women's names. Half of the name pairs are male names and half female.

For each name pair, *one* name has been randomly selected as the target member of the name pair. What you are asked to do is to go through the list of 64 name pairs, *underlining* just one name from *each and every name pair* to indicate which names you feel are the target names. Go through this test quickly. It should only take you a few minutes. Don't think too hard about any particular guess.

After you've finished, go back through the list and put a small cross by the side of any name in the list which is of significance to you – names of close friends, family, etc.

Again, please answer the questions which follow the test.

1 Tim	Bernard	8 Paul	Jim
2 Zoe	Doreen	9 Ray	Carl
3 Caroline	Dorothy	10 Bill	Reynold
4 Maria	Tina	11 Amelia	Fiona
5 Kevin	Eddie	12 Susan	Patti
6 Inga	Joan	13 Edna	Liz
7 Marilyn	Janine	14 Virginia	Eileen

15 Elizabeth .... Dora
16 Judy.....................Carol
17 Mary...................Diane
18 Walter .... Mark
19 Arthur.............. Nigel
20 Angela................Alice
21 Fred .... Andy
22 Jo .... Sally
23 Margaret .... Geraldine
24 Charlotte........ Brenda
25 Amanda ....Valerie
26 Peter....................... Ian
27 Tom .... Hugh
28 David .... Philip
29 Linda .... Yvonne
30 Donald...............Steve
31 Arnold .... Edward
32 Joyce .... Barbara
33 Nicki .... Sarah
34 Andrew .... Judas
35 Gerald .... Julian
36 Michael............... Neil
37 Helen ....Imogen
38 Sophie........ Susannah
39 Nick .... Alex

40 Harry .... Dick
41 Martin.....................Gary
42 Wendy .... Maggie
43 Colin ....John
44 Karen .... Teresa
45 Patricia ....Vicki
46 Oliver...................Simon
47 Barry ....Rick
48 Trevor.................... Keith
49 Adrian.............. Geoffrey
50 Richard............Malcolm
51 Justin .... Rex
52 Terry.......................Sean
53 Andrea .... Rachel
54 Mick...................Charles
55 Frank ....Tony
56 Mandy..................Jacqui
57 Hannah......................Sue
58 Christopher .... Robert
59 Patrick .... Brian
60 Laura .... Dinah
61 Rod.....................Graham
62 Jane ....Erica
63 Anna .... Vanessa
64 Christine................Anne

Questions
Tick one answer only for each question.

1 How relaxed did you feel when you did this test?
   Very relaxed
   Quite relaxed
   Neither relaxed nor tense
   Quite tense
   Very tense

2 What was your general mood like when you did this test?
   Very good
   Quite good
   Neutral
   Quite bad
   Very bad

3 How confident are you that you have used ESP in this test?
   Confident I've used ESP
   Feel it's likely I used ESP
   Uncertain
   Don't feel I used ESP
   Certain I didn't use ESP

On what date did you complete this test?......................

What time of day did you complete this test........am/pm

Test 3
This test is different from the others in that it is a picture-guessing test. Overleaf is a blank space – PIC-TURE – and for this there is a target drawing of some kind which you are asked to try and form impressions

of by ESP. The drawing could show almost anything, so this is a test where your imagination is given free rein. For this reason, it's a good idea to do this sometime when you know you'll be undisturbed, and settle down to relax and clear your mind of distractions.

The procedure is:
1 Prepare for a picture-guessing session; relax.
2 Try to get impressions of what the picture shows.
3 Try to make a drawing in the appropriate box showing the major features of the images and impressions you receive; if you can't, that's all right but you must complete Steps 4 and 5 (and do that even if you do make a drawing).
4 Write a brief description of your dominant images or impressions.
5 Reply to the questions about which features you feel were, or were not, in the picture.
6 Finally complete the questionnaire on mood, relaxation, etc.

PICTURE

DESCRIPTION

Questions
Underline one answer in each case.

1 Did the presence of people of any kind figure in
   your impressions?

   Yes, strongly/ Yes/ Not certain/ No/ Definitely not

2 Did the presence of colour(s) of any kind figure in
   your impressions?

   Yes, strongly/ Yes/ Not certain/ No/ Definitely not

3 Did the presence of animals of any kind figure in
   your impressions?

   Yes, strongly/ Yes/ Not certain/ No/ Definitely not

4 Did the impressions you received seem, for the most part, to come from scenes indoors or outdoors?

Definitely outdoors/ Mostly outdoors/
Equal (or uncertain)/ Mostly indoors/
Definitely indoors

5 Did you at any time, when receiving impressions, sense the presence of water of some kind – rain, a river, the sea, etc.?

Yes, strongly/ Yes/ Not certain/ No/ Definitely not

Questions
Tick one answer only for each question.

1 How relaxed did you feel when you did this test?
  Very relaxed
  Quite relaxed
  Neither relaxed nor tense
  Quite tense
  Very tense

2 What was your general mood like when you did this test?
  Very good
  Quite good
  Neutral
  Quite bad
  Very bad

3 How confident are you that you have used ESP in
  this test?
  Confident I've used ESP
  Feel it's likely I used ESP
  Uncertain
  Don't feel I used ESP
  Certain I didn't use ESP

On what date did you complete this test?.....................

What time of day did you complete this test?......am/pm

Reading about Psi*

General

The general field of parapsychology is covered by the present authors in *Explaining the Unexplained* (Prion 1995). Another general introduction is a book published by Aquarian Press in conjunction with the Society for Psychical Research: *Psychical Research*, edited by Ivor Grattan-Guiness. For people interested in the technicalities, there is the *Handbook of Parapsychology*, edited by B. B. Wolman, which is the standard reference work, but is hard going for the ordinary reader.

A book which takes in parapsychology only peripherally, but which explains important issues in the difficult and perplexing study of consciousness and the mind in an easily followed manner is Gordon Rattray-Taylor's *The Natural History of the Mind*.

* As many of these titles do not have American publishers, USA readers may find that books are available only in libraries with extensive collections in this area.

Finally, on the history of parapsychology up to 1914, there is Brian Inglis's *Natural and Supernatural*. Hopefully, Inglis will bring the subject up to date in a later volume.

ESP Research
The first two books noted above cover this field. Other good reads are *Dream Telepathy* by Monty Ullman, Stan Krippner and Alan Vaughan that discusses a long-term study in New York. This book is splendidly written and full of fascinating examples and anecdotes. *Mind-Reach*, by physicists Russ Targ and Hal Puthoff, discusses experiments on long-distance ESP or 'remote viewing' as they term it. Lyall Watson's *Supernature* is full of stimulating ideas, and is racily written, but do beware of some sources quoted in it!

PK Research
Kit Pedlar's *Mind Over Matter* is perhaps ill-titled since it covers more than just PK, but it covers both research and implications of P. K. John Hasted's *The Metal Benders* is a detailed account of his pioneering research into PK metal- bending; and for those who enjoy controversy, there are *The Geller Papers* edited by Charles Panati. The book *Frames of Meaning* by Harry Collins and Trevor Pinch is also a must.

Other researches
With only this space available all we can do is indicate just some notable books in special areas of parapsycho-

logy. *Poltergeists* are discussed in the definitive book of that title by Alan Gauld and Tony Cornell, and apparitions by Andrew MacKenzie in *Apparitions and Hauntings*. Mediums are discussed by Gauld in his *Mediumship and Survival* and the career of the most remarkable medium ever studied – the Victorian D. D. Home – by noted biographer Elizabeth Jenkins in *The Shadow and the Light*. There is no single book which covers the issue of survival after death comprehensively but in this context Michael Sabom's excellent *Recollections of Death* should not be missed.

On somewhat more subjective levels, Rosalind Heywood's *The Infinite Hive* and Michael Bentine's *The Door Marked Summer* both deal with personal accounts of psi and its role in life. On this wider issue, John Randall's super *Parapsychology and the Nature of Life* tries to integrate psi into natural science, while Hilary Evans in *Intrusions: Society and the Paranormal* looks at psi in society.

Appendix 1

Table 1

NUMBER OF GUESSES	NEGATIVE PSI			CHANCE SCORE
	p = 0.001 Excellent −	p = 0.01 Good −	p = 0.05 Some −	
6	−	−	0	3
7	−	−	0	3.5
8	−	0	−	4
9	−	0	1	4.5
10	−	0	1	5
11	0	−	1	5.5
12	0	1	2	6
13	0	1	2	6.5
14	0	1	2	7
15	1	2	3	7.5
16	1	2	3	8
17	1	3	4	8.5
18	1	3	4	9
19	2	3	4	9.5
20	2	3	5	10
25	3	5	7	12.5
30	5	7	9	15
35	7	9	11	17.5
40	9	11	13	20
50	12	15	17	25
52	13	16	18	26
60	16	19	21	30
70	20	23	26	35
80	25	27	31	40
90	29	32	35	45
100	32	36	39	50
110	37	40	44	55
120	41	45	49	60
130	45	49	53	65
140	49	54	57	70
150	54	58	62	75
160	58	63	67	80
170	62	67	71	85
180	67	72	76	90
190	71	76	80	95
200	76	81	85	100

Continued on page 178

Significance table for 1 in 2 – red/black card colour-guessing

POSITIVE PSI			SIGNIFICANT DIFFERENCES		
p = 0.05 Some +	p = 0.01 Good +	p = 0.001 Excellent +	p = 0.05 Some +	p = 0.01 Good +	p = 0.001 Excellent +
6	–	–	3	–	–
7	–	–	3.5	–	–
–	8	–	–	4	–
8	9	–	3.5	4.5	–
9	10	–	4	5	–
10	–	11	4.5	–	5.5
10	11	12	4	5	6
11	12	13	4.5	5.5	6.5
12	13	14	5	6	7
12	13	14	4.5	5.5	6.5
13	14	15	5	6	7
13	14	16	4.5	5.5	7.5
14	15	17	5	6	8
15	16	17	5.5	6.5	7.5
15	17	18	5	7	8
18	20	22	5.5	7.5	9.5
21	23	25	6	8	10
24	26	28	6.5	8.5	10.5
27	29	31	7	9	11
33	35	38	8	10	13
34	36	39	8	10	13
39	41	44	9	11	14
44	47	50	9	12	15
49	53	55	9	13	15
55	58	61	10	13	16
61	64	68	11	14	18
66	70	73	11	15	18
71	75	79	11	15	19
77	81	85	12	16	20
83	86	91	13	16	21
88	92	96	13	17	21
93	97	102	13	17	22
99	103	108	14	18	23
104	108	113	14	18	23
110	114	119	15	19	24
115	119	124	15	19	24

Continued on page 179

Table 1 – *continued* from 176

NUMBER OF GUESSES	NEGATIVE PSI			CHANCE SCORE
	p = 0.001 Excellent −	p = 0.01 Good −	p = 0.05 Some −	
220	85	90	94	110
240	93	99	104	120
250	98	104	109	125
260	103	108	113	130
280	112	117	123	140
300	121	127	132	150
320	130	136	141	160
340	139	145	151	170
350	143	150	156	175
360	148	155	160	180
380	157	164	170	190
400	166	173	179	200
500	212	221	227	250
600	259	267	275	300
700	305	315	324	350
800	352	363	372	400
900	400	410	420	450
1000	447	458	468	500

Table 1 part II *continued* from 177

POSITIVE PSI			SIGNIFICANT DIFFERENCES		
p = 0.05 Some +	p = 0.01 Good +	p = 0.001 Excellent +	p = 0.05 Some +	p = 0.01 Good +	p = 0.001 Excellent +
126	130	135	16	20	25
136	141	147	16	21	27
141	146	152	16	21	27
147	152	157	17	22	27
157	163	168	17	23	28
168	173	179	18	23	29
179	183	190	19	24	30
189	195	201	19	25	31
194	200	208	19	25	32
200	205	212	20	25	32
210	216	223	20	26	33
221	227	234	21	27	34
273	279	288	23	29	38
325	333	341	25	33	41
376	385	395	26	35	45
428	437	448	28	37	48
480	490	500	30	40	50
532	542	553	32	42	53

Table II

NUMBER OF GUESSES	NEGATIVE PSI			CHANCE SCORE
	p = 0.001 Excellent –	p = 0.01 Good –	p = 0.05 Some –	
3	–	–	–	0.75
4	–	–	–	1
5	–	–	–	1.25
6	–	–	–	1.5
7	–	–	–	1.75
8	–	–	–	2
9	–	–	–	2.25
10	–	–	–	2.5
11	–	–	–	2.75
12	–	–	–	3
13	–	–	0	3.25
14	–	–	0	3.5
15	–	–	0	3.75
16	–	–	0	4
17	–	–	0	4.25
18	–	–	0	4.50
19	–	0	–	4.75
20	–	0	1	5
25	–	0	1	6.25
30	0	1	2	7.50
35	0	2	3	8.75
40	1	3	4	10
50	2	4	6	12.5
60	4	6	8	15
70	6	8	10	17.5
80	7	10	12	20
90	9	12	14	22.5
100	10	14	16	25
110	12	15	18	27.5
120	13	17	20	30
130	15	19	22	32.5
140	17	21	24	35
150	19	23	26	37.5
160	21	25	28	40
170	23	27	30	42.5
180	25	29	33	45

Continued on page 182

Significance table for 1 in 4 – suit-guessing

POSITIVE PSI			SIGNIFICANT DEVIATIONS		
p = 0.05 Some +	p = 0.01 Good +	p = 0.001 Excellent +	p = 0.05 Some +	p = 0.01 Good +	p = 0.001 Excellent +
3	–	–	–	–	–
–	4	–	–	–	–
4	–	5	–	–	–
4	5	6	–	–	–
5	6	7	–	–	–
5	6	7	–	–	–
5	6	8	–	–	–
6	7	8	–	–	–
6	7	9	–	–	–
7	8	9	–	–	–
7	8	9	–	–	–
8	9	10	–	–	–
8	9	10	–	–	–
8	10	11	–	–	–
9	10	11	–	–	–
9	10	12	–	–	–
9	10	12	–	–	–
10	11	12	–	–	–
11	13	14	–	–	–
13	15	16	5.5	–	–
15	16	18	–	–	–
16	18	20	6	–	–
19	21	24	–	8.5	–
23	25	27	–	–	–
26	28	30	–	–	–
29	31	34	–	–	–
32	34	37	–	–	–
34	37	40	9	–	15
37	40	43	9.5	12.5	15.5
40	43	47	10	13	17
43	46	50	10.5	13.5	17.5
46	49	53	11	14	18
49	52	56	11.5	14.5	18.5
52	55	59	12	15	19
55	58	62	12.5	15.5	19.5
57	61	65	12	16	20

Continued on page 183

Table II *continued* from 180

| NUMBER OF GUESSES | NEGATIVE PSI | | | CHANCE SCORE |
	p = 0.001 Excellent –	p = 0.01 Good –	p = 0.05 Some –	
190	27	31	35	47.5
200	29	33	37	50
220	33	37	41	55
240	37	42	46	60
250	39	44	48	62.5
260	41	46	50	65
280	45	50	55	70
300	49	55	59	75
320	53	59	64	80
340	58	63	67	85
360	62	68	73	90
380	66	72	77	95
400	70	77	82	100
500	92	99	105	125
600	114	122	128	150
700	136	144	152	175
800	159	167	175	200
900	181	190	199	225
1000	204	214	222	250

continued from 181

POSITIVE PSI			SIGNIFICANT DEVIATIONS		
p = 0.05 Some +	p = 0.01 Good +	p = 0.001 Excellent +	p = 0.05 Some +	p = 0.01 Good +	p = 0.001 Excellent +
60	64	68	12.5	16.5	20.5
63	67	71	13	17	21
69	73	77	14	18	22
74	78	83	14	18	23
77	81	86	14.5	18.5	23.5
80	84	89	15	19	24
85	90	95	15	20	25
91	95	101	16	20	26
96	101	107	16	21	27
103	107	112	17	22	27
107	112	118	17	22	28
113	118	124	18	23	29
118	123	130	18	23	30
145	151	158	20	26	33
172	178	186	22	28	36
198	206	214	23	31	39
225	233	241	25	33	41
251	260	266	26	35	44
278	286	296	28	36	46

Table III

NUMBER OF GUESSES	NEGATIVE PSI			CHANCE SCORE
	p = 0.001 Excellent −	p = 0.01 Good −	p = 0.05 Some −	
20	−	−	−	3.33
24	−	−	0	4
30	−	0	−	5
36	−	0	1	6
42	0	1	2	7
48	0	1	3	8
54	1	2	3	9
60	1	3	4	10
72	2	4	6	12
84	3	5	7	14
90	4	6	7	15
96	4	6	8	16
100	4	6	8	16.67
120	7	9	11	20
150	9	12	15	25
180	13	16	19	30
200	15	19	22	33.33
240	20	24	28	40
270	24	28	32	45
300	28	32	36	50
330	32	37	41	55
360	36	41	45	60
400	41	46	51	66.67
500	55	61	66	83.33
600	69	75	81	100

Significance table for 1 in 6 – dice PK test, sevens test

POSITIVE PSI			SIGNIFICANT DEVIATIONS		
p = 0.05 Some +	p = 0.01 Good +	p = 0.001 Excellent +	p = 0.05 Some +	p = 0.01 Good +	p = 0.001 Excellent +
8	9	10	–	–	–
9	10	11	–	–	–
10	11	13	–	–	–
11	13	14	5	–	–
13	14	16	–	–	–
14	16	17	–	–	–
15	17	19	6	–	–
17	18	21	–	–	–
20	21	23	–	–	–
22	24	26	–	–	–
23	25	27	8	–	–
24	26	29	–	–	–
25	27	29	–	–	–
29	32	34	9	–	–
35	28	41	10	13	16
41	44	47	11	14	17
45	49	52	–	–	–
52	56	60	12	16	20
58	62	66	13	17	21
64	68	72	14	18	22
69	73	78	14	18	23
75	79	84	15	19	24
82	87	92	–	–	–
101	106	112	–	–	–
119	125	131	19	25	31

Table IV

NUMBER OF GUESSES	CHANCE SCORE No PSI	NEGATIVE PSI		
		p = 0.05 Some +	p = 0.01 Good +	p = 0.001 Excellent +
10	1	4	5	6
20	2	5	7	8
30	3	7	8	10
40	4	9	10	12
50	5	10	11	13
60	6	12	13	15
70	7	13	14	17
80	8	14	16	18
90	9	15	17	20
100	10	17	19	21
110	11	18	20	23
120	12	19	21	24
130	13	21	23	26
140	14	22	24	27
150	15	23	25	28
160	16	24	27	30
170	17	25	28	31
180	18	26	29	35
190	19	27	31	34
200	20	29	32	35

Significance table for 1 in 10 – number-guessing card tests

NUMBER OF GUESSES	CHANCE SCORE	NEGATIVE PSI		
		p = 0.05 Some +	p = 0.01 Good +	p = 0.001 Excellent +
220	22	32	34	38
240	24	34	37	41
250	25	35	38	42
260		36	39	43
280	28	39	42	46
300	30	41	44	48
320	32	44	47	51
340	34	46	49	53
360	36	48	52	56
380	38	50	54	58
400	40	53	56	61
500	50	64	68	73
600	60	75	80	85
700	70	87	91	97
800	80	98	103	109
900	90	109	114	121
1000	100	120	125	132

Table V: Random numbers

The numbers given in the table are between 0 and 9 inclusive, i.e. 10-way random digits. They can be converted into other types of random digit easily enough by the following methods. For example, when choosing one picture from a set of four (labelled 1, 2, 3 and 4) you need 4-way random digits. The list below shows how to adapt the 10-way digits for this purpose.

2-way: Take 1, 3, 5, 7, 9 = 1 and 2, 4, 6, 8, 0 = 2

3-way: Take 1, 4, 7 = 1: 2, 6 = 2; 3, 7 = 3; 4, 8 = 4. Ignore 9s and zeros.

4-way: Take 1, 5 = 1; 2,6 = 2; 3, 7 = 3; 4, 8 = 4. Ignore 9s and zeros.

81326	69493	17252	56488	89136	04859	04950	15899	09008	94274
41794	96056	81384	91697	81667	77633	93774	75967	70272	20556
18595	77056	28394	20501	89249	59570	16739	60939	34532	40578
18912	55185	86798	49547	56613	14601	19166	29291	79001	21207
06965	94664	16784	64299	40436	04945	09852	13450	70160	00693
78053	05077	79991	58124	91780	44904	72561	29267	66321	59460
67956	75343	54728	81153	51168	97263	47773	08783	72460	62860
07184	12416	97275	42361	45633	91508	62691	23829	20180	77967
38575	61363	81232	63821	65628	70282	49073	70574	30150	05421
21552	13511	41864	67198	88957	77364	28132	70330	44686	13413
56102	08260	09889	15283	57365	68677	24110	66961	48656	23209
90499	57054	60659	22926	13473	54528	99690	54571	34483	49861
66523	62117	87439	36685	42541	16566	24851	55375	52510	36817
13253	31477	11972	10739	21867	71743	80063	17745	29851	03300
04041	35097	34734	90188	26367	50871	50678	23516	11067	02106
60668	75930	22550	42813	85759	63125	72863	52363	62360	97143
57955	57163	11768	16961	73495	22582	58731	27067	46844	97531
73095	89167	98110	24924	62722	22939	24549	41936	48603	38513
60089	66406	94510	04161	91827	56556	19514	40979	02380	85780
95452	60185	37014	85540	91178	79501	16424	75373	35429	21459
11591	63910	87333	17774	50447	54148	39999	42533	76305	54553
23339	15609	16210	68406	47046	33565	98203	03391	19984	99543
84192	12752	69706	92869	86215	93542	41669	81888	88829	67122
24711	18015	71395	36485	89966	38286	78365	00758	22709	53130
01468	07063	01666	72043	92652	30615	73453	01825	12267	37760

5-way: Take 1, 6 = 5; 2, 7 = 2; 3, 8 = 3; 4, 9 = 4;
5, 0 = 5.

6-, 7-, or 9-way: Simply ignore digits outside the range
you need.

The table contains 2500 random numbers. You may
need extra random numbers at some stage, in which
case you can either consult a different table of random
numbers (which can usually be found in a text on statistics) or generate new sequences from the table here by
reading down columns instead of across rows, reading
sequences backwards or diagonally.

73087	30594	88381	84635	28198	55819	04803	24373	34697	09570
71230	90945	60824	10792	91067	68253	29253	61691	49159	19536
62370	04918	96462	22707	41561	36903	06759	10287	77910	68738
70118	38861	28510	04858	77255	37041	78607	93278	46733	93484
86523	13705	54182	78195	86961	94582	48019	32702	75312	57369
13029	58900	15773	51991	88232	42478	49216	21916	82875	97671
88082	98281	02444	20805	34414	19898	67192	69650	30909	67857
41852	04711	66181	26616	72482	31231	63290	12277	93218	94595
89742	26074	06714	41856	92343	76785	04041	97552	48939	02396
23596	99608	31224	71480	29786	33175	44141	22068	53653	72128
31106	83320	67156	37992	28821	64343	27625	08925	14205	73302
34876	15979	58456	76227	25723	36492	53417	40546	25234	94727
35051	02751	97426	36598	47118	27823	84038	07021	53975	92623
22256	83623	98420	60190	87851	31923	82638	22041	40413	88235
75861	46755	10204	30144	27249	58743	16102	30288	75130	93136
17309	44258	19667	47956	01798	52942	24755	81385	81242	34443
43485	40935	72080	01308	12843	43858	76936	48492	97348	78295
20337	18392	62064	46481	98806	33175	20399	76132	44962	68198
71172	64079	43662	29791	98753	98343	08019	23490	08656	04353
26409	30686	72645	84022	40254	92806	21687	06818	62286	58833
69414	42193	23901	84803	87822	14704	33584	23214	13433	37260
17878	58736	30195	34534	67673	71115	95234	06884	40579	89515
45236	10153	60986	10909	90998	37561	61590	59902	92143	69557
07636	03808	44859	98203	72053	07958	00789	98590	30419	52839
20944	79089	37296	41353	60438	75053	57536	00241	85793	39506

The Z test

The Z test can be used to calculate the probability of a result from any type of forced-choice ESP test using a hit or miss scoring method (which you will need to do if the number of guesses you make in a test is not found in Tables I–IV). Thus, card-guessing and PK test results can be scored using the Z test, but picture-guessing sum of ranks results cannot (see Chapters 5–7). The Z test can be used for any number of guesses, with any chance hit probability (1 in 2, 2 in 3, 1 in 4 and so on), except when the number of guesses is small.

$$Z = \frac{(\text{actual score}) - (\text{chance average score})}{\sqrt{[N \times P \times (1-P)]}}$$

N is the number of guesses and P is the chance of being correct by chance with a guess. So, if the test is a 1 in 2 test, $P = \frac{1}{2}$ or 0.5; if the test is 1 in 4, $P = \frac{1}{4}$ or 0.25; and so on. The chance average score is easily worked out: in fact, it is $N \times P$. You will need a calculator with a square-root function to work out the bottom line of the equation. See p. 154 for a worked example.

What do various values of Z mean? Although the derivation of Z is beyond the scope of this book, it can be shown that if Z is 1.96 or greater, the results are significant when $P = 0.05$; if Z is 2.58 or greater, the results are significant when $P = 0.01$; and finally if Z exceeds 3.30 then the results are significant when $P = 0.001$.

Finally, two technical points about Z. First, the Z test is not statistically reliable if $[N \times P \times (1-P)]$ – the denominator – is less than 9. Under such conditions, the number of guesses is probably small, and so the tables in Appendix 1 will be more use.

Second, some statistical authorities recommend that if the actual score is greater than the chance average, 0.5 should be subtracted from the numerator; if the actual score is less than the chance average, 0.5 should be added to the numerator. This always makes Z somewhat smaller and so results that appeared significant before may not be when this amended procedure is adopted. This adjustment is called a continuity correction.

The sum of ranks test

This statistical test is for use with rank-sum results from picture-guessing tests (Chapters 5–7). It can be used for calculating the significance of results from any number of trials, or using any number of rank judgements for each guess (four picture alternatives as suggested in the text, or more, although the same number of ranks must be involved for all guesses!).

Before giving the formula, two technical points should be noted. (This test does give a Z value and is a form of Z test, but to prevent confusion, we term it the sum of ranks test). First, this test should not be used if the number of guesses is less than 25; second, a continuity correction, as given above may be used, although it is not used in the examples given below.

$$Z = \frac{(\text{actual sum of ranks}) - (\text{chance average sum of ranks})}{\sqrt{[N(R^2 - 1) \div 12]}}$$

N = number of *guesses*
R = number of *ranks*, and R^2 is R multiplied by itself; so if
$R = 4$ then $R^2 = 16$.

Again,
if Z is 1.96 or greater, then the results are significant when $P = 0.05$;
if Z is 2.58 or greater, the results are significant when $P = 0.01$;
if Z is 3.30 or greater, the results are significant when $P = 0.001$.

Example

A subject completes the heroic total of 92 trials, with a four-way picture-guessing test. The sum of ranks is 209. Is this significantly different from chance?

With a four-way ranking test the chance average rank is 2.5; so for 92 trials the chance sum of ranks is $92 \times 2.5 = 230$. The score we found was 209, a deviation of -21 from chance (so the score is better than chance).

$$Z = \frac{209 - 230}{92 \times 15 \div 12}$$

$$Z = -21 \div 115$$

$$Z = -21 \div 10.72$$

$$Z = -1.96$$

This value of Z is exactly what one needs for significance at the $P = 0.05$ level. Note, however, that if we had used a continuity correction, the value of Z would be 1.91 and not quite significant. So this outcome should be interpreted cautiously.